AFTER SUICIDE

"You know when you lose someone like this it's like a big chunk of yourself, you know?" "The first month I used to wake up at night screaming for my husband." "Well, you tell yourself then, you know they were sick and [with] something they wouldn't be able to live with. So they suffer, they finish suffering, you know, suffering no more." "And I remember saying over and over, 'Oh my God! It's all my fault, it's all my fault.' I just kept saying this over and over again, and . . .'" "Even my mother kept saying, 'We'll have a hard time telling our relatives that . . .'" "Oh——I felt, uhh——pity, you know, such ——I felt such uhh, uh, pity in my heart, you know, I, it was——I mean my heart was, you know, I uh, it was bad——I mean my heart was, was really broken——I just felt so——so BAD . . ." "It was like, uh, a bad dream——but it was really, uhh——a terrible, a terrible, terrible experience." "I should have known something was wrong."

AFTER SUICIDE

Samuel E. Wallace

A WILEY-INTERSCIENCE PUBLICATION

John Wiley & Sons, New York · London · Sydney · Toronto

Library of Congress Cataloging in Publication Data:

Wallace, Samuel E
  After suicide.

  "A Wiley-Interscience publication."
  Bibliography: p.
  1. Suicide—Case studies. I. Title.
  [DNLM: 1. Suicide.   HV6545 W194a 1973]

HV6545.W34   364.1'522   73-9793
ISBN 0-471-91865-2

Printed in the United States of America

10 9 8 7 6 5 4 3 2 1

To Susan Mervin

FOREWORD

MODERN SOCIOLOGICAL RESEARCH may be said to have begun with the study of suicide that Emile Durkheim published in 1897. It was the first study to assemble a mass of empirical data about a social phenomenon for primarily theoretical purposes. After an exhaustive analysis of how suicide rates varied over time by nationality, religion, occupation, and marital status, from town to country, by age and sex, and by other social characteristics Durkheim concluded that "suicide varies inversely with the degree of integration with the social groups of which the individual forms a part." He then went on to make more general inferences about how our happiness depends on collective processes of which we are scarcely aware.

Ever since Durkheim showed that the study of suicide could be used to illuminate the machinery of social cohesion, such studies have flourished. A bibliographical investigation commissioned by the National Institute of Mental Health almost concurrently with its sponsorship of Professor Wallace's research, discovered 3469 books and papers on suicide and suicide prevention published in the 70 years following the appearance of Durkheim's book. Not all of these made any theoretical contribution, of course, but a good many of them did, and the general drift of their findings is that suicide is associated—at least statistically—with the absence or loss of important social relationships.

Professor Wallace has worked very much in this tradition in electing to study twelve Boston women whose husbands committed suicide at about the same time in order to understand in each case the influence of the marital relationship on the suicidal act and the effect of that act on the widowed survivor.

The results of this inquiry, as the reader is about to find for himself, are consistent with Durkheim's theory that men are protected from suicide by the marital relationship; in more than half of Wallace's cases an emotionally overloaded marriage had finally broken down just before the suicide occurred, and in all the remaining cases the husband's physical or mental disorders had gravely interfered with the marital relationship.

Thus the findings of this study tend to confirm the findings of many predecessor studies and to underscore the dependence of human creatures on their close associates, not only for happiness but even for the will to exist. But in some other ways *After Suicide* is a highly innovative work, original both in its methods and in its results.

Confronted with the news of a suicide, whether a friend's or a stranger's, we ask almost reflexively "Why did he do it?" To this reasonable question, a statistical study of suicides can give only an uncertain and speculative reply. Durkheim, for example, identified the principal types of suicides as egoistic, altruistic, and anomic. But his data, which consisted of suicide rates for various populations during various intervals of time, gave him no way of estimating how many suicides of each type occurred in a given population and no way of classifying an individual suicide. On the other hand, the many case studies of suicide published by psychiatrists tell us very little about the social phenomenon, since we have no means of appraising the typicality of an individual experience. Professor Wallace has devised a research format that seems to me to combine some of the merits of a statistical analysis with most of the advantages of a case study. The sample of cases is admittedly small but it is essentially random and, provided that the data show sufficient consistency and we are not too demanding about the level of statistical significance, it is possible to draw tentatively valid conclusions from such a sample. At the same time, the power of the case study method to discover the experience behind the bare statistic is enhanced by dividing the experience of each respondent before and after her husband's suicide into meaningful stages and comparing her action and sentiments at each stage with those of other widows at the same stage. Each segment of experience is illuminated by comparing it with a range of parallel experiences, and I think the reader will find that the dramatic impact of the narration is unexpectedly increased by the presentation of variations on the same theme in different lives. The sole difficulty is that one sometimes loses track of the speakers. But even if some haziness surrounds these narrators, the force of their quoted words is extraordinary. Like a few other notable pieces of sociological writing— William Whyte's *Streetcorner Society* and Oscar Lewis' *Children of Sanchez*, for example—Wallace's *After Suicide* can engage the emotions of the reader as effectively as a novel or a play. What it lacks in literary contrivance, it makes up in verisimilitude. The characters seem real to us because, in fact, they *are* real, and they enlist our sympathies because skillful observation and interviewing has revealed them to us as if we had met them face to face.

This new kind of literature—literary but not fictional—derives its impact from the heightened sense of reality it conveys, just as a good novel conveys a heightened sense of reality because the author's imagination enables us to understand the actions of other people. A research report such as *After Suicide* gains a similar quality by virtue of an enormous input of carefully gathered information. There is always a risk, of course, that such a project will fail because of inadequate theory or the inaccessibility of information, but when it succeeds, as in this book, doors open in every direction.

THEODORE CAPLOW

University of Virginia
Charlottesville
June 1973

CONTENTS

AFTER SUICIDE

ON COPING

COPING WITH SUICIDE is coping with death, and although death always takes its toll, suicide extracts even a higher price, threatening the very lives of the living. When the suicide was your spouse, an already intense experience is further intensified. "One's not half two, it's two are halves of one," * halves of one relationship a man and a woman formed with each other "to have and to hold from this day forward until . . ."—until he chose to leave her behind. Whether that conjugal relationship thrived on love or disintegrated into hate, each spouse was one of two. In life as in death, the suicide and the conjugant left behind are inexorably drawn together. What life had joined not even death could put asunder.

Life and Death are also two "halves of one"; that is the second message of this book. Beginning with life, we will

* E. E. Cummings, *Complete Poems 1913–1962*, by permission of Harcourt Brace Jovanovich, Inc.

then observe experience with death, returning afterward to the encounter with life. Our concern is with life, with the living who also inevitably experience death.

Life and death in husband and wife—these are intense experiences within an intense relationship. On this stage, grief will be seen in its most severe form. Why should anyone search out these encounters with Hell? Because we have created this Hell through which we shall now pass; because it cannot be changed except from the other side; because to prevent or alleviate this intense grief requires persons with an understanding of its causes.

Twelve women whose husbands committed suicide tell of their lives as they experienced death. Wherever possible their story is told in their own words, the words they used in the one hundred and four interviews we had with them during the first year after the death of their husbands.

Their experiences with death by suicide varied widely, and I found I had to add what I call *social death* to make their differences understandable. For although some reacted with the intense grief we might well expect, others responded with a sigh of relief, an attack of "conscience," even a stream of invective. Their responses to death varied, as had their responses to life. And in their lives, some of these twelve husbands were dying socially long before their physical death.

There is physical dying and death, and there is social dying and death, and we may or we may not react to either form of death with the feeling of loss. "I only regret I didn't do this ten years ago," Mrs. Miller told her husband when she separated from him. Any "loss" she experienced thereafter was welcomed—"it's so peaceful around here." She saw to it that he went out of her life, died socially for her. His physical death two years later did not leave her grief stricken.

People leave our lives in a variety of ways and we may

or may not miss them. To expect otherwise, to consider physical death alone as departure, is to create a straitjacket for our emotional selves.

These observations and more are contained within this study of twelve women whose husbands committed suicide. They told us of their lives in the nearly monthly interviews we had with them over the year. The average time of each interview was two hours; the shortest was thirty minutes and the longest lasted four and one - half hours. Most interviews were tape - recorded and fully transcribed. The transcriptions filled several thousand pages —half a file drawer. This voluminous documentary file is referenced first by the fictitious name assigned to the widow, then by the number of months after her husband's death in which she told us what is quoted, then by the number assigned to the interview, and finally by the page number of the interview transcription. This important information given at the end of every section quoted should therefore be read as follows, using the manuscript's first quotations as examples: in "I was born in Canada. . . ." We are quoting Mrs. Morneau, who told us this two (2) months after her husband died in our first (1) interview with her as found on page three (3) of the interview transcript—that is, MORNEAU 2.i.3. The next quote is from Mrs. Burke five (5) months after the death of her husband in our third (iii) interview with her as found on page ten (10)—BURKE 5.iii.10. The reader will find this contextual information invaluable in understanding such critical processes as the widow's recovery movement, the progressive impact of this research on her, and even the intradynamics of an individual interview, since the page number tells the reader approximately when in the interview a remark was made.

Observed behavior is noted in parentheses—(laughs), (cries), (softly). Occasionally words have been added in

brackets to clarify the speaker's meaning. Words the
widow emphasized are capitalized. The words (not clear)
mean that a word or two could not be understood at that
point on the tape recording. Italicized comments in parentheses were made by the interviewer. Ellipses indicate
omissions from the narrative. Dashes indicate pauses. The
longest ——— indicates a long pause. A pause is indicated by a dash of this length: ——. A short pause is indicated by the shortest dash —. The interviewer's
questions are in italics and are not set off in quotation
marks. Within a widow's remarks, italicized comments in
parentheses were made by the interviewer.

Extreme care was taken in accurately transcribing all
tape - recorded interview material. The same care has been
taken in reproducing that material here. To *hear* these
women as they tell us about their experience in being widowed through suicide, the entire manuscript needs to be
treated as written oral literature. It should be read slowly,
word for word, even aloud.

After Suicide begins where those women began, with
their lives before meeting and marrying their husbands.

LIFE BEFORE DEATH

THE TWELVE WOMEN whose husbands were to commit suicide began their lives like many other women. Their fathers were farmers, skilled craftsmen, businessmen, professionals, and were present in all but three families where divorce and desertion had taken place. Their mothers for the most part were housewives, Catholics, Protestants, and Jews of various intensities. Only one of the women was an only child; most had both older and younger siblings. Only two were born outside the United States, one in Canada and one in Ireland.

"I was born in Canada, but I was the only one of my sisters who was born there. My family came from Canada but they moved to Fitchburg for a while, and that's where my sisters were born. Then they moved back to Canada when I was born. My sisters and my mother are still there. My mother is ninety - two years old and lives in a nursing home." (MORNEAU 2.1.3)

BIRTH AND ADOLESCENCE

The widows' fathers were reported to be widely varied in temperament, as were their father's fathers.

"I had a strict father. He did too. I think that's why he was strict. I can remember back to my high school days. I never went anywhere, I never went to the dances. My mother wasn't [strict], my father was. I remember my mother always covered up for what time we came in. My father was strict, when I went to parties, I always had to come in early, you always feel funny—I always had to leave before anyone else—and I was grown up. I was twenty - four when I got married. And my father was strict." (BURKE 5.III.10)

Three of the women lost their fathers through divorce or desertion.

"My mother had a very hard life bringing up five children; my father died, uh, left my mother, he just walked out to work and that's it, and we were all very small. She just had her burden on earth, that's all."

Did this shake your confidence?

"I was only little, I don't even remember my father at all. My sister was only about twelve or thirteen, she was the oldest, and I was in the middle, so I imagine I was only about six or seven; you don't remember, I just don't remember. I don't know if I don't wanna remember, or if I just don't remember, I don't know." (Sullivan 5.iv.9)

Only one of the fathers had died during his daughter's childhood, and in a single other case the mother had died while her daughter was young.

How old was your dad when he died, how old were you?

"Uh, I was twelve. I think he was forty - two."

How'd he die?

"He had a heart attack."

Did he have a bad heart for a while before that?

"Yeah, he had trouble with his blood, it was clotting or it was too thick and uh, he was on medication and um, he was getting well—and he was all right then, and he had no problems at all, and he hadn't gone to the doctor, and he was really coming out of it, and he just felt fine. And then all of a sudden . . ."

He went very quickly, then?

"Umm. He went in his sleep, he was sleeping, or it was at night—and it was spooky (giggles)."

How did this affect you and your mother?

"Umm, well like—uh—it's awful to say, but it affected my mother—like she has a grudge, and um, like she's always saying 'You know I'm the mother and the fa-

ther in this house.' You know, I think she holds a grudge
—and I don't even know who she holds it against . . ."

How did this affect you—to lose your dad?

"Uh, it hurt. And it still does hurt. . . . The family was
very close, and after he died it was uh—you know, we
all felt it—every one of us." (AGO 7.III.34)

Another woman in effect lost her father because of the
death of her mother.

"I didn't live with my father. I lived with my grandmother and my aunt after my mother died. Well of course
the first thing I missed out on having a mother, you know,
although my grandmother and I were very close and she
was very good to me. I was her favorite grandchild. But,
umm, I sort of felt left out like when other grandchildren
were there. I, uh, my mother wasn't there and usually my
father wouldn't be there and——" (BANKS 4.II.12)

Some of the women were from small families, others
were from larger ones.

". . . No. I was, uh, my mother was uh, I was a meno-
pause baby, really. My mother was forty, uh, what the
heck was it? (Figures out loud but unintelligibly.) She was
forty - two when I was born, you know. And I was the
youngest of twelve——seven living. . . . so that, uh I
never remember my mother as a young person. I always
remember my mother as a short, chubby, tired woman.
She always worked between babies. My father, uh, rarely
worked. He always complained of stomach problems, you
know." (TIBBETTS 9.VIII.34)

When they went to school, none of the women reported unusual difficulties, although one reported being "boarded out" quite unexpectedly.

Did you have a bit of trouble getting through school?

"Yeah, in the first four years of school was the most difficult."

How come?

"Well, they put me in the first grade of public school, first, I couldn't do nothin'. They told my father I had to go to special schools. My father wouldn't hear of it because he went to special schools himself. He wouldn't hear of it. So then my mother said, 'Well, why don't we put her into parochial school?' They tried that, and I was all right for the first year, second year, third year—and then they put me in the orphanage the third year. And that was a little difficult."

In an orphanage?

"Yeah, in an orphanage. My mother was sick at the time. They put my brother in too, he was six—my father didn't want us runnin' the streets while he was working, so he said, 'You're better off.' " (SLOAT 12.VI.28)

Mrs. Jefferson reported continuing but unexplained difficulties with her parents.

. . . you said jail just now?

"Oh, that's the reformatory."

That's what you meant as jail?

"Yah, see, in there, it's for juvenile [offenders]. . . . You have to go to bed earlier and you're not allowed the privileges as if you are in jail, but it's a hell compared to jail, making jail a heaven."

And how come you were there?

"Because I ran away (laughs). Uh, one time, like I went back and forth, uh, one time I was in court and the judge, uh, said I could go home and my mother stood up and said I don't want her and all this shit so I got sent back and I chased her all the way down the hallway (laughs). I would have killed her (laughs)."

Had you run away several times before they did this?

"Oh, yah."

Where did you go when you ran away?

"Oh, mostly New York. Uhh, that's where I met, uh, the first time I really left this state I was eight months in New York and we met Art and Sue there. Art and Sue acted, are like my true family and anyway they taught me so much more than my real folks ever did. You know, they couldn't even comprehend what was being taught." (JEFFERSON 6.III.38–39)

All except one of the twelve women left home to marry before reaching the age of thirty, the exception staying at home to care for her aging and now alone father. Her mother died when she was nineteen.

"You know when you're the last one in the family and you're not married, and you've only got one parent, everyone expects you to stay with this parent. Particularly if you're a female." (TIBBETTS 11.IX.8)

As they told us about their childhoods, not a single differentiating pattern emerged. Some of their families were intact, others were not. Some seemed beset by problems, others not. While not all of them remembered growing up surrounded by love, only one woman seemed to evidence apparently severe psychological problems.

"I suffered REALLY ever since I was in high school, with insecurity and anxiety complexes at different times and, uh, which is—it had a pretty bad effect on the family at times because I would actually go to bed and not be able to get out of bed sometimes, and not, not be able to carry on at certain times——normal patterns——. . . . I started with this first when I was in high school, and I had a real, real bad time of it then. It was directly after the death of my grandmother and I don't know WHY it was then, but it was. But my mother and father were divorced when I was five, and ever since I was a little girl, really, I've had the pattern of insecurity and anxiety . . .
". . . the doctor——they didn't know too much about——emotional problems at that time. And the doctors thought because I, I'd faint, or I thought I was going to faint when I'd go into restaurants and this sort of thing ——I kept thinking I was going to faint and pass out and I'd cry and they'd have to take me out, and they'd have to take [me] in the car and all this sort of thing. . . . It was my emotions that were. . . . I think, you see, I had a very insecure childhood——my, my mother is a——is an emotionally unstable person and a periodic drinker, which

made me extremely nervous, and uh, I'd lay in bed at night and pull the covers over my head and cry." (GRENON 11.VIII.25–27)

Consequently, all that can be said of our widows' lives before they married is that with the exception just cited they were not apparently unusual.

MARRIAGE

Ten of our women met and married their only husbands at normal ages, all but one before age thirty and in quite predictable patterns.

"Well, like I said, I was . . . you know, real strong headed. I would just go, you know, I'd say, well I'm going to the library and I'd, uh, go, uh, uh, go out with the girls, you know. So that I had to——any time that I went out I had to sneak out and they had a uhh, what was it——twenty-five year anniversary at the, uhh, lakefront and they had all these ships from all over, uhh, Coast Guard cutters on display. They had beautiful, uhm, flags and what - have - you and they had painted—— they had about twenty - five of them, and I don't remember what we went in town for, and there was a sign there and it said come and see the open house, come and see it. So we went on in and that's how I met my husband." (BANKS 4.II.30)

The Burkes met in the civil service while she was typing for him; the Agos, Banks, Grenons, and others were from their respective same small towns. Some of the women described their first meeting with their soon - to - be husbands in typically glowing terms.

When you first met each other, how was it then?

"Oh, it was beautiful [meeting Phil]. I was living with Manny, and I was the only one working. Oh, God, Manny—he's the laziest I've ever met in my life and Phil was working in the mailing department where I was and, like all we did was, we didn't even talk, all we did was smile at one another all day, it was cute—(laughs)." (JEFFERSON 5.II.20)

Others claimed more external influences.

"I married him for security—isn't that a laugh? It was not just a cold - blooded selection of a mate—he was attractive to me, he was a sweet, wonderful guy. Also, it was wartime—it has quite an effect on gals—you feel that you've got to get married. He was going into active duty. Officer's training school, about to go. ——After all, I was dating all this while; after all, I was 22, practically an old maid (laughs)." (GRENON 4.III.18)

Two of twelve lost their first husbands—one was killed in action in World War II, the other was lost to a very good, long - time friend and neighbor. Both of these women had children from their first marriages.

Again, with one exception their reasons for marrying and general courtship patterns are far from unusual.

"We met on a blind date. And we just went out. You know, it was just, uh, he was different from the other fellows that I went out with. And I guess, that, more than anything else was why. He was quieter; he just didn't mix; he was always very clean; you could see yourself in his shoes. He always had a nice hair cut and his pants was ——he was just neater in appearance."

*Any guys before you met him that you perhaps were in
love with? . . . or perhaps liked a lot?*

"I went with one, gee, it was about three years. And we
had an argument and then I went out on a blind date with
Doc. I remember he called me up and I just wouldn't go
out with him. And I started goin' out with Doc."

*How long did you go with your husband before you
were married?*

"Umm. About a year. A year and a half. That's all."

Considered marriage for that length of time?

"No. Uhhh, the marriage part was that we went up to
New Hampshire, uh, his brother and his wife was gettin'
married. His wife was Protestant and her family was
against, you know, gettin' married, with a Catholic. 'Cause
William was a Catholic. They ran away and got married
and while they were up there gettin' married; we did
(laughs)."

Then you eloped?

"Yeah. Yeah. I didn't tell my mother for three months
(laughs). I wouldn't tell her; she'd kill me (laughs). I just
remember that Doc fought with me for three months
(laughs). 'Tell your mother; tell your mother.' And finally I
told her and I run (laughs). I didn't see her for eight
months."

*How was it that your mother didn't find out that you
had gotten married? Were you living with your mother at
that time?*

"Oh, yeah. Yeah. Yeah."

You mean you continued living with your mother?

"Oh, yeah, for three months (laughs). I wouldn't tell her—(not clear)—she'd tear up the marriage license. . . . I——I got married——I don't know why I did it. I have no idea to this day why I did it. Doc said, 'Do you wanta get married?' I says 'No, I don't want to get married.' And the next thing you know I was getting married." (SULLIVAN 4. III. 33–35)

Their lives were so predictably normal at this stage that everyone, of course, thought that the yet - to - be Mrs. Sullivan had eloped because she was pregnant.

Nor was Mrs. Zack's manner of choosing a mate unusual.

"When I was in high school my parents wouldn't let me go out with anyone who wasn't Jewish. I sometimes think my marriage to Lester [a Catholic] was a reaction to my parents. I was a real REBEL when I was a kid, you know, in school. And if they said black, I did white. You know, and um, I, I think to some degree I was really rebelling. I didn't go out with ANYONE who was Jewish when I went away from home." (ZACK 9.III.45)

Mrs. Zack is not even unusual among our twelve women. Witness Mrs. Tibbetts.

Did you ever date anyone of French nationality?

"Absolutely not, I didn't [that is, didn't date them] just to be ornery. . ."

Did you ever meet anyone that you could have considered dating that was French?

"Not particularly, because most of them were my relatives." (TIBBETTS 9.VIII.21)

Ordinary lives in ordinary families, meeting and marrying normal males—the pattern of normality continues through their husbands' trades, occupations, and professions.

Mr. Banks was an industrial electrician and was employed regularly until two or three years before his death. "He didn't even need an alarm clock to wake him. He was in very good physical condition—and he was a handsome man. He always made a good appearance. Didn't he, Fran?" Fran, her daughter, who was present during this first interview, answered: "Yes, he was a stunning man."

Mr. Burns was a government employee, Mr. Codman an industrial chemist. Mr. Grenon was on the way to becoming a communications executive, and Mr. Zack was a student at a high prestige professional school. Among the twelve men, only one was often unemployed; that couple was supported by his parents.

THE NEED FOR CARE

It is only when we turn to examine the broad category of care needed that the pattern of normality is broken. Five of the twelve grooms had to have, or at least thought they had to have, special care from some other person. And all of the five women knew of these care needs before they married their husbands. The care they needed differed in several dimensions as it did in its manifestations, yet the need for care was undeniably present.

"Chicks didn't dig him at all because he was, you know sort of deformed, I guess you would say. He'd had polio when he was very young and one of his legs was withered and it was a messy thing to see. . . . I found out that he was an unwanted child. I always felt I had to sort of guard him against things, and you know, he always wanted children and he was really—he felt very sad when we weren't having any children. And then his mother told me when we were there that he was sterile. It's from when he had polio he was sterile. He didn't know it though and I didn't tell him. I never told him." (JEFFERSON 3.1.6)

The second groom's need for care was necessitated in large part by the impoverished environment in which he lived. With adequate medical care his condition probably could have been controlled and thus his future transformed. Without competent medical attention, however, his need for care could only intensify.

"Yeah, his mother had told me about it. I had known, she told me that he had a seizure every year, but it was more than that."

Your mother - in - law told you that?

"Well, he had mentioned that he had epilepsy and had a seizure a year, and his mother had said the same thing." (SLOAT 4.11.6)

The "seizure a year" turned out to be at least weekly, one occurring just before the marriage at her parents' house. Somehow she managed to convince them that it wasn't what they thought, a ruse she continued until "safely" married. Given the scarce medical attention available in our society to so many like Mr. Sloat, inevitably he had seizures at work and was fired, adding employment to his growing list of needs.

Three other husbands had "nearly visible" problems—at least their women knew fully of them before their marriage. Mr. Ago became addicted to cough syrup at age fifteen. By age seventeen, three years before he married, he had graduated to heroin. Why would anyone knowingly marry a three - year heroin addict? A previous relationship of Mrs. Ago's helps explain.

Have you been hurt in some way that you could tell me about?

"Um . . . that kid John that I went out with for five years."

What happened to break you two up? Was this an instance when he did something to hurt you?

"He said, at my brother's wedding, 'Won't it be nice when we get married?' You know, he scared me."

Really? That sounds like a compliment.

"He was really pushing getting married and I just wasn't ready to get married."

How old were you then?

"Uh, nineteen. He scared me."

Was he the same age?

"No, John's around twenty - two, he's a couple of years older than I am. And, he really scared me. I almost went

'Hey, groovy. Getting married! Hey, John.' But then I saw my brother and his wife in the actual ceremony, and I figured Billy's not coming home anymore to live at the house, he's going to be living with Marie. I don't want to live with John all the time—forget it." (AGO 7.III.50)

After that "hurt," Mrs. Ago does appear to have looked for and found a mate with whom she could remain a child.

"Oh it was just fine. I just enjoyed being married."

Everything about being married?

"Yes, it was just quite an experience, it was like a big game—you know? Like we were playing house together, and, uh, I really enjoyed it. I really enjoyed being married. All good things have to come to an end."

What other things did you have going for you? What sort of interests did you have in common?

"We liked to do—like, I like to do a lot of stupid things, and he did too. Just spur of the moment things. There wasn't any one particular thing because Bobbie and I were very much alike. We like to do the same things. Anything. We always ended up laughin' about it."

What sort of things? Could you tell me some of these things that you liked to do?

"One time Bobbie thought I was getting fat, so we went for a walk and—I don't dig walkin' at all, and he doesn't either. And we were out for about three hours, and it was freezing out, and we were enjoying ourselves (laughs) walking, because we were fooling around as we were walking. Stepping on the cracks, and breaks my mother's back and all. . . . It seems that everything we did—we had fun." (AGO 7.III.48)

So the Agos played house while living with and being supported by his parents. No doubt the Agos are unusual in their pattern of mutual dependency, yet theirs is not a pattern that would lead one to suspect possible later suicide.

Mr. Tibbetts, the fourth care - needing groom, had the extreme misfortune to be part of the United States Army when our Pacific front fell in 1942. He was eighteen at the time and spent the next forty - two months in a Japanese prisoner - of - war camp. Then in a series of operations lasting nearly three years, a large section of Mr. Tibbett's stomach was removed, his tuberculosis was brought under control, and his "nerves" were somewhat calmed. Upon release from the military hospital he quickly became an alcoholic, reportedly with his first wife as company.

How did you meet, you and your husband?

"It started way back. . . . With his first marriage he had an awful lot of problems, you know. . . . And when he went away to [the hospital for his TB] she said right to his face 'I hope you die,' that she hoped he'd die. . . . Apparently when he went into the hospital this other man had moved in. He lived with her in this apartment with the five children. Pat was really upset about this and he didn't know what to do because you know, this is no way to bring up children. So he . . . made a request to be transfered to [a hospital closer home]. We were all pretty close—the staff and the patients—you knew who was infectious [with TB] and who wasn't, so we had our own Ping - Pong table and our own pool table. You got to know their personal problems. When he left I said 'Now be sure and write. I want to be sure you go to [another institution].' . . . he left us in July and in the end of August I stopped by to see if he was there. Just out of curiosity. He was, so I said 'Gee I'm glad to see you're here.' So I said, 'Do you mind if I come and see you once in a while?' . . . once or twice he asked me if I would mind taking him to see his boys in Brockton. I said 'Absolutely not' and this was all there was to it. . . . It sort of grew; it was nothing flourishing. And all of a sudden we were much younger." (TIBBETTS 3.III.13)

Mrs. Ago knowingly married a heroin addict, Mrs. Tibbetts a former POW, now an alcoholic with TB. Yet only Mrs. Codman married a predictable candidate for later suicide, predictable because Mr. Codman had tried to commit suicide twice before.

Just before his ex-wife remarried over his vigorous protests, even though she had moved out of state, Mr. Codman made the first serious attempt on his life. The attempt put him into a coma for five days, from which he finally emerged completely paralyzed. Because he had no one else visiting him, the soon-to-be Mrs. Codman did so "as a friend."

"I went twice a day every day for a long time and still he would call me just because he needed the security of knowing that there was somebody who cared." (CODMAN 4.II.18)

After an unspecified period of time, Mr. Codman was flown back to Milwaukee where his parents could care for their middle-aged son. They kept in touch, then she drove out to Wisconsin to visit him and meet his parents. While she was driving west he attempted suicide for the second time. Despite this second attempt and all the implications of its timing, Mrs. Codman took Mr. Codman for her second husband.

Five of the husbands needed special care prior to their marriage. Their soon - to - be wives knew of their condition and the special care it would require of them: Ago had to have more "junk" or another "cure"; Sloat needed medicine and care during seizures; Jefferson had the constant pain of being polio crippled and needed at least some assistance; Tibbetts needed many medicines, health, and the bottle; and Codman was both paralyzed and in need of constant watch lest he try to commit suicide again.

By accident or by the force of something deep within them, five of the twelve women set up housekeeping with men who were already out of the ordinary in this significant respect. In only one case, however, that of Mr. Codman, were there unmistakable grounds for fearing later suicide.

Given this realistic risk, why did Mrs. Codman marry him?

". . . I think that I sometimes, well, not resent it, but felt pressured by the strength that he was looking for which, of course, was really what brought us together anyhow. But, you know, he use to have an expression, 'You're a tough little nut.' Boy, I got tired of being 'a tough little nut.' He thought I could handle anything. I didn't feel that I could handle anything. Not anything, and not everything. ——Gee, about six months went by and if, if he actually fell in love with me it was then, it was after we were married. And I'm not sure, I'm really not sure why he decided that we should marry. I'm sure he wanted to, maybe it was almost a feeling of, 'What else can I do? I want a, I want as normal a life as I can have. No one else is going to marry me. She cares.' I'm not sure that this wasn't an awful lot of it."

If you had to choose between you and Irving, in terms of the desire to get married, which would it be? Were you more interested?

"—— (softly) I think me."

Keeping in mind that we had talked to Mrs. Codman about herself for nearly sixteen hours in nine interviews over the year, listen now to her explanation of what brought them together.

"I think he found me as a very strong person. And being able to handle almost anything. And I think I probably saw in him someone who needed me very much. Which my first husband obviously did not. And I can't imagine, even looking back I can't answer specifically, but I can't imagine not responding to that kind of need——a very strong need. When someone needs you, you, you just automatically respond to them. If you like the person, anyhow, uh, you, you're bound to get involved."

Yes. But at the same time—

"And I needed to be needed. There was no question about it."

Okay. But the question then becomes, at what risk? Did you think in terms of at what risk you would respond to this need? To yourself?

"No. I DID NOT! I DID NOT! And it was a tremendous risk. I did not! I absolutely refused to even look at it.—"

You see this now, in retrospect.

"Yeah . . . and here I am sitting back in the situation that exists today and I'm looking SPECIFICALLY at the risk. . ."

How about . . . when he had attempted suicide in January? What was your response then to the risk of responding to this need? (Mrs. Codman clears throat.) *To yourself as well as to him?*

"Um, I was scared. I was scared and I was going through with it. I refused to accept it. I ABSOLUTELY refused to accept it. Which obviously, which obviously was pretty difficult (very softly)."

Because of the compelling nature of the need that you felt?

"Uh - hum. Uh - hum. The compelling nature? I found that I was very much in love with him at the time and refused to see it."

And that would be the next question. Why did you marry him?

"I loved him——I refused to look at it. I wouldn't talk to anyone about it; nobody knew about it; uh, his, his parents were the only ones that knew. I never told a soul and I still never can. Only his parents and his sister knew anything about it [the suicide attempt]. I simply refused to accept it . . ."

Can you look back at Mrs. Codman then? With what observations?

"THAT'S a good question. . . . ———— There was a
TREMENDOUS compelling need there. Uh, everything else
was kind of hinged on it." (CODMAN 15.ix. 15–16)

The need for care became joined to the need to care.
For these men needed special care; their wives especially
needed to give care.

THE NEED TO CARE

"You gotta watch 'em real careful. I sez to him, that morning, don't you take your bath 'til I get up. It was really
early and I was still sleepin'. But you know men, they
think they gotta be real strong and no one tell 'em, no
woman tell 'em what to do to take care of themself. Char-
lie was that way (smiles). He was real strong. He was a big,
healthy lookin' guy. To look at him you'd say to yourself,
gee, he's a real healthy guy, he could never be sick a day in
his life. And he liked to play ball, loved to play with the
kids in the neighborhood. I'd worry one day he'd be
playin' ball, and he'd get gripped up with a seizure, fall
over and a car'd run him over." (SLOAT 2.i.3)

As we have learned, special care was needed for five of
the twelve grooms. Now our exceptionally care - giving
research volunteers tell us of seven more husbands needing
special care, these needs manifesting themselves after marriage. The length of time between marriage and the ob-
servable time of needing special care varies from a few
months to a quarter century. It also varies as to precisely
when it could be said that the husband needed care. Nevertheless, the need reached out.

The need that cast its shadow earliest in all the relationships was that of the Banks.

"No, I usually don't have an appetite. I don't feel like eating."

Oh, I see.

"That usually happens when I'm nervous or upset and I'll get that."

And you've had this, what? Since you were married, did it start?

"That's when I found out. I was married about three months when I found out I had it. . . . By that time I knew my marriage wasn't going to be what I expected it to be." (BANKS 10.v.10)

". . . he could hold his liquor—— Uh, you know, he never got drunk—he never. It was, uh, one, two weeks before we were married he met me. . . . He met me at the bus stop and he was sort of drunk—that was two weeks before we were married.

". . . that was the first time I, you know, that I had ever seen him really drunk. And it kind of knocked me for a loop, you know, you know——and I said—I looked at him and I said, 'Have you been drinking?' And he said, 'Oh, a little bit' but you know, I could tell by his eyes. And I said, 'Oh,' I said, 'You're drunk.' I said, 'I'm not going anywhere with you tonight.' . . . That was the first time, two weeks before we were married, that I'd ever seen him really drunk."

And what did you think about it. Did you——?

"It scared me a little—you know, it did."

Why did it . . . ? Did you have some suspicion that it was a problem, or—?

"Uh——yah I did. Uh, well I don't know if I had any suspicion but I didn't like it. . . . It just didn't seem to me —I was dis—let's say, I was very disappointed—very disappointed in him. . . . Umm, but it, uh, it was a disappointment; it was a terrible disappointment for me. . . . I said, 'Oh, God.'— I mean I don't know—because I was in a neighbor—I lived in a Polish neighborhood and, like, about fifty percent of the men that lived in the neighborhood—I mean they used to—we called them beer joints back home and, you know, they'd go in there on payday night and they'd come home—swaggering drunk and then fighting with their wives; I didn't want any part of that—but that's what I lived with for over twenty years."

Did you ever think in that two weeks of maybe not getting married?

"Well I'll tell you, I went—you know, I was happy as a lark before that—but that kind of like, sort of cast a shadow."

Did you talk to him about it any more or was there ever any . . .

"(interrupts) No. No. I didn't think—no, I didn't think I should. No—I didn't think I should bring it up, and I didn't."

Were there any other episodes like that before you got married?

"No."

And then when did the drinking problem first show itself?

"Well like, it wasn't, uhh, see, you know, like it wasn't a problem in the beginning. . . . Only on weekends at first. On a Friday night he would come home and he would have had a few—before he got home. . . . Saturday night it would be the same thing——well I'd say for the first, let's say, for the first two or three months—that's right, it was Friday and Saturday he'd get, you know, a good glow on. . . . Then, uh, he'd be late for dinner and he would be 'on his way' and that would continue Saturday. Then it would continue on to Sunday. Then it was just, you know, repetition. . . . But he wouldn't drink during the week. Then we came out here and that's when he really let loose." (BANKS 6.III.27–30)

Banks, Grenon, and Morneau began to commit suicide inch by inch through alcoholism. All three of them followed the predictable pattern of increasing consumption and decreasing health until alcohol took over entirely. This gradual deterioration sapped the life from drinker and spouse alike so slowly that both had difficulty recognizing the condition even when it had become obvious to everyone else.

Sullivan and Miller were disabled through work accidents. At thirty - seven, Mr. Sullivan, refusing any help, lifted some heavy equipment he used in his trade and severely damaged a spinal disc. An unsuccessful operation left him paralyzed from the waist down. He was never again able to walk without heavy leg braces and crutches, nor ever able to work again.

Mrs. Sullivan said her husband was not expected to survive the first operation; but having done so, he needed four or five others to correct adhesions. In the first eight years of his paralysis, he also returned to the hospital five other times for other problems. She stated that Doc was in constant pain, and that after the first few years he developed a tolerance for drugs that left him unable to sleep most nights. He got into the habit of going for a ride in the middle of the night in his especially equipped old car—it seemed to ease the pain.

"When he first got hurt? Well he was, uhh, he was mad on the world. When he first got hurt he didn't want to come out of the second operation after the first one. He tried in the FIRST one. When Doc was operated on I went to see him, he was so mad, fighting, and swearing and yelling and screaming, and the doctor said that's what made him come out of it. But he was so sick. Well, then six weeks later, uh, he got operated on. I went in; he was laying there like a—there was not a sound out of him. He opened his eyes and (not clear) he says, 'Humph, I didn't die' and he closed them again. He didn't want to fight after the second one. He just didn't fight at all after that . . ." (SULLIVAN 7.v.23)

It must have been very difficult for a man as active and all as he was, after the accident?

"Mm. . . . It was terrible for him. For about a year and half he wouldn't get out of bed or go out AT ALL. He was down to about one hundred and nineteen pounds and he was almost six feet tall. And the doctor told me I was killing him with kindness. [So] I told him I was gonna go out and get a MAN (laughs) and he could drop dead and I'd be a rich widow (laughs), and I went out the first night and he didn't follow me, but the second night he did. Hah. And then he started going out." (SULLIVAN 11.viii.10)

Unlike Doc's accident, Mr. Miller's seemed somewhat suspicious.

Could you tell me what happened right from the beginning of the day [of the accident]?

"Well he went to work—when I got—in the afternoon—I didn't have a telephone—(not clear)— my sister came up and she said, 'Mike fell down the stairs. They're taking him to City Hospital.' He was unconscious I guess when they took him. He slipped on a stairway. He had glasses, a pair of glasses in one hand and a can of putty or something in the other. But he got up and he walked down and he got downstairs and passed out. They called the police and took him to City. They only kept him there for a week and let him come home. Then he had his own doctor visit him and his own doctor sent him to [another hospital] and they couldn't find anything wrong there. So, uhh, then, uh, something come up with the conversation and he got a lawyer and the lawyer changed doctors . . ."

And he came home from City and went to bed?

"Yah. He had to spend most of the time in bed."

How did he get home?

"Uh, somebody gave him a ride home."

He was able to get in a car and come home?

"Yah. Yah."

How much do you think it was malingering, you know, making it worse than it was?

". . . Well, at first I didn't but then I said, well, nothin's very much wrong with him when he gets mad or gets drunk . . . He did say one day, 'It's gonna be a while before I will go back to work.' Of course, I figured he (not clear) I think he was trying to get a large sum of money out of that because that was one of his ideas."

Did he?

"Well, he got, uhh, some——but not as much as he expected."

How much did he get?

"Fourteen thousand dollars. He blew it. He went to Ireland."

Well, Mrs. Miller, he couldn't have been really too terribly crippled if he could make a trip back to Ireland.

"Well that's why I say, at times he was FINE. But I don't know."

And at times he had to use two canes to walk?

"Yah. Well after——after——I, I may be wrong, but I think he did himself more harm than good. He never even tried——he'd——he didn't try hard enough, I don't think, to get better. You know what I mean? (*Mmmm.*) I think you could make——you could make yourself sick if you wanted to . . ." (MILLER 9.v.45–50)

Mr. Burke did not require special care until he reached his mid-fifties and had supported others for a quarter century.

"My husband, a year ago, he had a terrible headache and was acting strangely, so the doctor examined him, put fluid into his brain, suspecting a brain tumor. Instead it was hardening of the arteries, but at a very early age. The doctor didn't tell me about it though, he kept it a secret, he knew that I am very nervous, that Joan [daughter] is very ill. . . . I only found out that Don had hardening of the arteries, that the main artery, what do you call it? that goes to the brain? was almost impassable, the blood couldn't go through it to take oxygen to the brain—from the psychiatrist I took Don to. . . . He couldn't understand what was going on in anything he would do—television, even the quiz shows he used to love—he was such a smart man, so intelligent, and then he couldn't even read the newspaper. He would bring it in each day and sit behind it, but I knew he wasn't reading. It took him an hour to read just three sentences." (BURKE 2.1.3)

"He forgot how to cook, he was the most marvelous cook you ever saw—he taught me how to cook. He loved to cook—and he was wonderful doin' housework, he could do anything, you know? And he seemed to forget—like to make a bed, he didn't make it right.

". . . about a month later I had a bad case of the flu and this was when it became clear that he was helpless. 'Cuz he made me go to bed . . . and I don't think he realized himself that he couldn't do it—and all he was makin' was hamburgers, and all of a sudden he was yellin' at me— 'Come down, I can't make them.' And I come down and here was a whole bunch of hamburgers all stuck in the thing. He didn't know what to do with it—he didn't even know to put it into patties—and this was when I realized something was wrong." (BURKE 8.v.5)

The twelfth and final case had only the misfortune of family history and experiences: when he was sixteen and living with her, his mother committed suicide upon being divorced. Did this require special care from someone? No doubt it would have helped him yet it is also true that his need for care was not of the same order as Mr. Codman's or even Mr. Jefferson's. Also, Mrs. Zack sought not to fulfill any compelling need.

"I'm lazy. That's the only honest way to describe me, just plain lazy——I just don't like work.

"To tell you the truth, I never liked school from the beginning. School for me was mostly a husband hunt. . . . My husband Lester I considered to be very bright, a great potential, which he was. I was just dying to get married even though I was having a lot of fun at Indiana, you know, a pretty girl, dating a lot."

Why did you want to get married?

"I think the idea was pushed in my mind to get married by my family, you know, go to school to find a husband, the middle - class mentality, and a child has nothing other to go on than what her family, her mother puts in her head." (Zack 10.iv.5,6)

Nevertheless, Mrs. Zack was soon to have her problems.

". . . when we met we probably weren't opposite. Although, I think it was a very (sighs) right from the beginning, it wasn't a good marriage at all, but uh, you know, I think I was, I was very young, I was very blind, I was very foolish and the kinds of problems that we had, I always said, 'Well, with time it'll get better.' " (Zack 9.iii.2)

"Oh, he was a real hypochondriac. He was losing his hearing. He was losing his vision." (Zack 12.v.9)

"And, uh, I really found that it was a very one - sided relationship. You know, uh, especially emotionally. He needed so much, uh, you know, strength and guidance and direction in everything that he really was a burden to me after a while; and he just drained me."

Were you aware of these demands when you first knew him and first met him?

"Um, no. I mean, I may have felt them. He had a lot of problems then. He was going blind, he was going deaf, I mean he was also very, hypochondriacal and uh, I was aware that, you know, like he was difficult, but, you know, I had no idea of how difficult it would be from day to day living, you know, for the rest of your life with a man like that. Uhm, and he just had no ability to give, to help, uh . . ." (ZACK 9.III.5)

Twelve seemingly ordinary women marry twelve men, of whom five need special care even before they married them: Ago the addict, Sloat the epileptic, Tibbetts the POW tubercular alcoholic, Jefferson the polio cripple, and Codman the twice would - be suicide. After marriage, alcoholism reduced Banks, Grenon, and Morneau to special need status. Work "accidents" felled Sullivan and Miller four to seven years later. Then a totally debilitating stroke destroyed Burke. An epileptic seizure got Sloat fired, bringing him completely into the special need category. Only Jefferson and Zack remained somewhat on the margin.

With what kind of care will their needs now be managed? By whom? And with what consequences? These are the questions we now ask our volunteer informants.

CONJUGAL CARING

The need for care coupled to the need to care—two halves of one relationship. The care needed and that which was given consisted of many things. "I protected Father," Mrs. Sullivan told us, by screening him from the problems of his children. She cared for him by protecting him from what others might say to him. "I worked two jobs so Lester would not have to ask his father or even the school for a loan," Mrs. Zack volunteered.

What was your life like right after his accident, that first year?

"It wasn't bad at all. He was really good because he was in the house and he was in bed most of the time and I took care of him, did everything for him. Then he had the operation and I thought he'd be better but instead he got worse because I figure the operation wasn't a success." (MILLER 9.v.34)

Giving that care sometimes required long dormant or quite new abilities from our conjugal caregivers.

"A year ago he was the boss, he managed this house completely, even the kids he controlled with the strictest discipline. I had to learn how to pay bills. I had never even written a check, and I had to balance the checkbook, and oh, that was so hard to learn, everything that he used to do. Everything I did I used to ask him about first, I needed his advice, I depended on him so. He always knew the answers to everything. Then when he got sick I had nobody, no one to take his place. I had to learn how to live all over, to be a different person." (BURKE 2.i.4)

Some of the women not only had to do less for their husbands than be a different person, they also took it more in their stride.

"He could not drive. . . . With the car, I think that was a terrible area for him. For a man to not be able to drive a car, that is a loss of independence for any man, and he could not drive. He did not yet have the coordination. . . . I had to drive because I had to drive. . . . I think he must have told me every time we went to Haverhill, how to drive. I knew perfectly well how to get to Haverhill, I never said a word, but just chuckled to myself, but for him that was his driving. 'Take a right here, and a left here, and a right here'—and we must have done it a hundred times (laughs)!" (CODMAN 12.VII.5)

"He couldn't." He couldn't do many things sometimes just because he couldn't.

"Well, I just try to tell him to stop to drink. That's all. What can I do? Nothing I can do besides that. . . . he always find an excuse. That, that's the alcohol, you have to find an excuse. So he always find an excuse."

What sort of excuses would he give you?

"He makes some when he don't have none. . . . I told him, I said, 'I know you want to drink, but,' I said, 'Please, Jim, don't try to make an excuse for it . . . Listen, you used all the excuses you can use. . . . I don't think you be able to find no more excuse. Why don't you agree you drink because you want to drink? You don't have no more excuse to drink. We don't say nothing to you. We let you do what you want so you can find no more excuse. Why don't you say to yourself I drink because I want to drink. I can't stop.' "

So what did he say?

"He said, 'I know. I know I can't stop. I know, I try.' I said, 'I know you try.' He said, 'I can't stop myself no more.' And that's right, he really couldn't. He was trying but he really—he couldn't do nothing for it, nothing he can do because we all try, we all talked to him and it didn't help. And he knows it; at the end he knows that they couldn't do nothing. He was hooked on everything; he couldn't do nothing. He didn't have the power and he didn't have the courage and he couldn't help himself." (Morneau 6.iii.32–33)

To be helped, to take care, to admit to fundamental human need, does produce dependency if only for the moment. When caretaking becomes extended to one's total life, however, it makes something different of the caretaker, as well as of the person giving the care. First note the tendency for the need for care to vary with its availability. The more care the wives gave, the more care their husbands needed.

Second, care given is responsibility taken. Thus as the care increased, so did the responsibility of these wives for their husbands. Whether his problem was in the bottle or in an accident, the wife's fortunes came to hinge on his outcome, to the measure for which they were responsible —that is, gave care.

Their families and friends acknowledged their success, when they had it, often doing their assigned part in her management—for she was responsible. Bound ever more closely to her husband's rise or fall, she tried even harder to make of him a success, naturally giving him even more care. While not all of the twelve women became so intimately involved with their husband's lives, this is nevertheless a theme that runs with varying intensities throughout these conjugal lives.

They also solved the management problem in different but related ways. One common process that had different manifestations was the deception that came to be practiced. "You had to watch out for him," "to protect him," "to not say things which might put him into his moods." Becoming the role that they were playing, it was only a short step to deceiving themselves.

"At one point, it looked like he was sincere about giving up the booze. I suggested that we keep only soft stuff in the house so he wouldn't be tempted but he said, 'Look, we can't do that to our friends, why be hard on them?' . . . and I believed him—that was my trouble—I always believed him and believed in him. (*Why?*) I cared for him. (*Why?*) He was such a nice guy—so gentle and loving—such a good father—but that's what the psychiatrist said—that he wasn't. He kept saying 'Why do you always say he is such a good father when he clearly isn't?' " (GRENON 2.1.6)

Mrs. Morneau was quite emphatic on the subject of protecting her children's image of their father.

Do they know that he saw women or anything like that?

"No, no, no. No, I wouldn't tell my children that. No."

They have no idea?

"No, no. No, no, no. They don't, they don't have to know those things. I want them to know their father was a good father and I don't want them to know if he did something wrong, I don't want them to know. If he done something wrong, I don't want them to know that. That's no need for them to know those things. No." (MORNEAU 6.III.55)

Each wife varied in the care she gave her care - needing husband, just as they differed in the responsibility they took. Some screened their husbands almost completely from all others, some deceived only themselves. Benevolent as it was intended to be—care given, responsibility taken, and deception practiced—the consequences of this pattern soon proved to be disastrous for all concerned.

Another consequence of the care - responsibility - deception pattern was the conjugals' isolation from outside help. Pretending that things were better than they were made it difficult for them to seek help. The success of outsider help might also challenge the wife's own management of her husband's problems. Finally, success in our society is often thought to consist of what other people think, and some of the wives perhaps believed that no one would think well of them if outside help had to be sought. It was not that they were selfish, unconcerned, or subconsciously attempting to destroy their husbands. Their husbands needed care and they naturally responded by giving care to them. They themselves were then in turn influenced by these bonds, which they had helped forge.

CARE MANAGEMENT THROUGH SILENCE

In five cases, the women were already performing the role of caregiver before their marriage. They gave their care, as did the other wives who joined them, in three distinct patterns: confrontation, silence, and domination. Of these three modes of response, only Mrs. Sullivan and Mrs. Tibbetts confronted their husbands directly, and then only in the initial phase of their marriages. Silence and domination thus became the major patterns.

". . . I went from one boss [her mother] to another boss [her husband]. I figured that was his privilege. Then he went in the service; then I changed."

How—in what way did you change then?

"If he started a fight and (not clear) I told him to get out; I lived all the time he was in the service, I had a baby by myself, I took care of the house by myself and I didn't need him. And Doc almost dropped dead. Then Doc started to change. Then he got different; then we got along fine."

Did he tend to drink when you first married him?

"When we first was married, yah."

Then what happened about his drinking?

"Then he stopped."

Completely?

"Oh, he used to break out once a year or so. But, we'd have a fight and I'd tell him to get out and then he was all right and he'd stop; he wouldn't drink for six or seven months and then he'd start again. But, uhh, he completely stopped after a while; he really did." (SULLIVAN 3.II.11)

"But, uh, we fought and argued and yelled and screamed and eeeeeh, and he would end up walking out and I——

he'd come in and I'd throw a chair at him. 'You stay here and you finish the argument with me' (slight laugh). 'Or I will argue for months if you don't.' I use to throw anything I could get my hands on at him. I put a knife and it went right by him (laughs). And uh, after a while, he, 'Well, I guess you want to talk about it.' I said, 'Yes, I want to talk about it.' That took him a long time for him. . . . 'Cause Doc didn't talk, but he listened (laughs). He was a good listener for my talking." (SULLIVAN 12.x.15,17)

Whether Doc Sullivan would have become an alcoholic without the forceful reaction of his wife is anyone's guess. Regardless, her remarks underscore her husband - management practices and a type of management unparalleled in the other widows, except for Mrs. Tibbetts.

". . . at the beginning, it was, I, I wanted him, uh, you know, uh, I wanted, uh, see——try to control someone else's life is ridiculous——but this is what I was doing, I guess. I wanted to see that, he, he, continued with his treatment because he was improving; he wasn't infectious [with TB] anymore, you know." (TIBBETTS 9.VIII.28)

". . . as far as drinkin' I don't think I realized it, uh, you know I think he drank, I didn't know he drank to the extent that he did—I honestly didn't. If I want to believe what everyone, all the kids have said—I think he got quite violent when he drank—but, and it was always referring to the Japanese—plus the fact that when he did, I guess she [his first wife] did an awful lot of nagging. I'm not saying that I didn't nag when he drank at the beginning—but within six months he stopped, you know, and that was the end of that." (TIBBETTS 3.III.38)

How did he stop?

"I called the police on him (laughs). . . . He was very dependent at that time. . . . You know, I think he, he was, he had been such a lonely fellow, you know. And he had, uh, been so unhappy a good deal of his life that he, you know, he was looking for someone, you know, near him all the time. And I couldn't be here and, so this is when. . . . At that time I didn't even realize what it was doing to him."

Now what about your pouring the drinks down the sink?

"Well, this didn't help him. He got kind of provoked at this."

So what would he do when he was provoked?

"Well, he continued to drink."

Did he say anything to you? Did he curse you for throwing——?

"No. No. No, only if I nagged him. Then he would say, 'You're, you're like, you know, all the women, you're naggers.' Well, I said, you know. At that time I said he was comparing me to his ex, and I said, 'Don't you ever dare compare me to your ex - wife. . . . First of all I am not a drunk. Second, I am not a whore, you know.' "

And what would he say?

"So that would shut him up. He'd shut right up." (Tib-betts 11.ix.26)

"After bailing him out of jail we had coffee, so I said 'Do you still think you don't have a problem with drinking?' and he sez 'Yeah, I guess I do.' And I sez, 'What do you plan on doin' about it?' He sez, 'Well, what can I do?' I sez 'You can go to AA, you can take Antabuse, which is a pill, you know, or you can get hospitalized. If you are sincerely motivated, you know. These are three ways of doin' it.' " (Tibbetts 3.iii.38)

Doc Sullivan and Pat Tibbetts ·stopped drinking. Doc, however, was later to be felled by an accident at work, while Tibbetts's TB, strained health, and "nerves" continued to disable him. Even though they had other problems, excessive drinking was not among them.

Banks, Grenon, Miller, and Morneau also started or continued heavy drinking in the early years of their marriages. Their wives also became their caretakers, but with different care - management practices. Mrs. Morneau is illustrative of their basic pattern. The early years of marriage began quite predictably.

". . . one of my cousins used to go meet him and he used to go drink every Saturday night and came back when the barroom closed, one o'clock; so I let that go for a couple of Saturdays. Then I got mad and I told him; I said, 'I don't want that no more.' I know the wife of the other one don't like it either. So I said, 'That's gonna have to stop. . . . If you don't stop,' I said, 'I'm gonna call my cousin there. . . .' So they, he stopped that anyway ———." (Morneau 6.iii.37)

He then went elsewhere?

"Yes, because I remember. . . . I remember when the kids were small, you know, I try, even try, you know, to keep him home——he used to——he used to bring a bottle and I try to drink with him. One night I have three drinks with him—uuch, I was crazy, ooh, and after that

I never take three drinks (laughs). I remember one night, we always play cards, and I was drinking with him; I said, maybe if I drink with him he's gonna stay home (laughing). That was the only night (laughing)." (MORNEAU 14.VIII.18)

Unsuccessful in joining him as well as in stopping him from drinking, the husband's disease began to have an effect on their joint social life. Unpleasant drunken scenes that need no narration led the wife to stop inviting friends into their home, and their friends began to stop inviting them. The husband started avoiding everybody.

"Then he started to talk about wanting to travel. He wanted to get away from 'em so that he could drink whenever he wanted to. He took a low - paying job in order to learn the work he wanted to do. Because the money wasn't enough, I helped out by taking a night job. The AA told me that I was too easy on him, that I did the wrong thing and made it easy for him to get away and drink. I thought at the time that I was doing the right thing." (MORNEAU 2.I.13)

Mrs. Banks, Grenon, Miller, and Morneau reflect the same pattern with respect to the consequences of their husbands' drinking. They dealt with the problem in similar ways.

". . . every time I opened my mouth there was a—— there was an argument——and, uh, and, you know, and I wouldn't. Like it was a silent——household. . . . I wouldn't because I knew that everything . . . anytime ——no matter what it was. —— I never said anything, you know, I just kept my mouth shut . . .

"I used to tell Freddie, I said, 'When you come home from work, go in your room and stay in there until you know he's asleep,' which wasn't right either. Like I was, it was such a——it was a sick—sick—sick atmosphere for everybody."(BANKS 8.IV.21)

Mrs. Banks remained silent as did Mrs. Grenon, who retreated into herself as she had done during childhood.

"He didn't really want to be with them in the first place (laughs) and then, by having too much to drink, he would start turning on me, you know, to the point where I couldn't make a statement without him saying 'What do you mean—that's ridiculous.' And I'm by nature am not sure of myself, I mean I feel unsure of myself because I feel an intellectual gap with other people. So I'm not too sure when I go to make a statement anyway, and when someone is just sitting there waiting to pounce on me——[it] destroys me. So I figured that we may as well just hole in, pull the roof over our heads and just stay by ourselves." (GRENON 4.III.5)

Mrs. Moreneau firmly believed that she was better off not knowing too much about her husband and that he also was better off not knowing what she thought or felt.

"What do I care—I don't know the woman. What's done is done, but he didn't have to tell me."

Was it hard not to say anything to him, you know, about when he mentioned the woman? Did you have to keep yourself back from saying something to him about it?

"Yes, oh, yes, a lot of times. Yes, a lot of times."

You mean you would have really liked to say something?

"Sometimes—(laughs) yes, but I wouldn't dare."

Why wouldn't you? "Hmm?" *Why wouldn't you dare to say something?*

"No, he would—it wouldn't do nothing good; it wouldn't do no good, just make the things—to me, it'd just make the thing worse."

In what way would it make it worse?

"Because he wouldn't agree with me; he would never agree with me."

How about, would it help you just to let it out?

"Maybe, maybe at that time it would; I don't know. I really don't know."

Well, what would you do? Did you want him to think that you didn't think about it or didn't care?

"No. No. No." (MORNEAU 6.III.44)

Mrs. Morneau, Miller, Grenon, and Banks all remained silent. They tried to keep the peace through silence and in effect went along with their husbands' drinking. None of them threatened their husbands with actions like leaving or forcing them out. Mrs. Ago, who basically followed the same pattern of silence, said she tried threats but knew they were never believed and rarely acted upon.

"I tried to get him into Bridgewater, and to stay there long enough to do him some good, but no, he kept having his way. He'd go into the Medford Clinic for junkies where all they'd do is give out prescriptions for Methadone and more Methadone, and tranquilizers and sleeping pills that kind of thing that all it did was support the habit. It was a horrible place, all these junkies, real losers, all skinny and depraved looking, would sit there at the meetings, never listening to the instructions, just waiting their turn to get the Methadone and leave. . . . Bobbie did the same as the others." (Ago 14.vi.3)

"He kept having his way" is a statement that would fit the five cases thus far, that way being largely unopposed. These five stand in contrast to the five who slowly or from the outset took over their husbands along with their problems. At least they thought they did.

DOMINATION THROUGH CARE

Did he seem to be a weak man?

"No."

In any way before?

"No. He ran the house; he was the head of the house in his own way, but he didn't know what I was doing behind his back (laughs). He thought he ran the house! Imagine! Yah."

Were you actually running the house in your own way?

"Always. Always. (Laughs.) Yah." (Sullivan 3.ii.38)

Another one of the five women who took over their husbands said she first wanted to help him get back to his first wife and family.

"On the first of July he was supposed to sign himself in State [hospital]. And I knew he lived [nearby]. So I says, well, I'd better check up on him. But I didn't check up on him until August. Just out of curiosity. I said, well, I'm going to check up to see if he's there. And sure enough he was there. I was really pleased, you know, because I thought, Jesus, now this guy, maybe he can get, you know, back with the family." (TIBBETTS 9.VIII.30–32)

In a third example of the "taking him over" management style, the wife said everyone went to great lengths to protect her husband.

"One thing my brother done, he knew there was no other choice, he went down to the unemployment, with my husband, he'd got in line in front of my husband, so he talked to the person first. And he'd told the woman, 'His wife don't want him to work. Because she's applying for ADC for him and the baby, he's got epilepsy, and he got hurt in the foundry'—explained the whole story about —so they said okay. And they gave him a paper to go for his job, my husband, and my brother the same paper. My husband went with him, so they'd call and say they only need one man, and the first one we'll hire—the first one in the alphabet. Which was my brother they hired, and they told my husband we'll call you. But the woman at the social security had contacted them, and had given him the piece of paper to make him feel good. 'Cuz she didn't know what else to do. But he didn't want to hurt him." (SLOAT 12.VI.31)

Thus Mrs. Sullivan, Tibbetts, and Sloat "took over," as did Mrs. Codman and Burke. Five styles of silence and five women who took over: of the two remaining, one virtually ignored her husband's need for special care, in part because she married him for her own special reasons.

"And then we came back here and I wouldn't have gotten married. I didn't want to get married. But two reasons, my folks were going to throw me back in the Detention Home I was in once before, and I didn't dig that scene."

Why would they do that?

"Because of my living with a guy and not being married to him [she was under eighteen] and they can do that. And also I told my husband that I didn't love him; I shouldn't say love; I really didn't dig him as much as the other one, and I told him honestly. And I said, 'If you want to accept it that way, get married that way'——I told him also I didn't believe in getting married. I said, 'Will you take it that way?' He said, 'Yes, I accept it. I will accept it.' But, I guess he did; I'm not sure." (JEFFERSON 3.1.4)

In the twelfth and final case the husband was "castrated and dominated," to use Mrs. Zack's words.

"I became very, very dominating, very castrating I suppose. I mean because, you know, if something had to be done, Lester would never do it. And instead of, and perhaps to a certain degree, if I had been more confident in him, maybe this would have helped him too, you know, uh, but instead of sitting back and saying, I know Lester can handle it. . . . If I didn't do it, it wouldn't get done. Whatever it might have been. . . . It seemed everything he did, just didn't work out. You know. And I just lost, you know complete confidence in his ability to do anything. I paid the bills. I did everything because he couldn't, I felt he couldn't do anything. Now, perhaps to a certain degree my feelings might have created some of that. I mean, that's very possible. I tend to think that it was the other way . . ." (ZACK 12.v.5,6)

Whichever way it was, such management practices differ in part from those of Mrs. Tibbetts who controlled so kindly, or Mrs. Sloat who protected so thoroughly. We are therefore left with two major patterns of husband care - management practices, and two special cases that are related to the major patterns. In every one of the twelve cases the women practiced the same management patterns from the start to the end of their husbands' need for special care. As we have already learned, five started before marriage, and only Mrs. Sullivan and Mrs. Tibbetts changed from direct confrontation to taking over. As we shall later learn, the end of the husbands' need for care will vary. In the limit placed upon their care as well as throughout their lives with their husbands, the wives' management patterns are evident.

We have already wondered why these women gave so much care for so many years. Since five of the twelve were well into the caregiving pattern before marriage, and four more began it shortly thereafter, they apparently were responding to a need deep within themselves to give care. Caregiving led to the giving of more care, to the assumption of increasing responsibility for their husbands, to their own management practices for them, and to the increasing identification of their selves with the objects of their care. Within this context they could continue to give care, even when it seemed that the husband himself did not care.

Care at what price? Even when the person cared for doesn't care? Even when he abused and deeply hurt the giver of that care? What is the price of caring?

THE PRICE OF CARING

Ago's heroin, Bank's alcohol, Burke's stroke, Codman's paralysis—all of the problems of the twelve husbands were conditions that isolated both husband and wife, and isolated them increasingly as time went by. First to go were their friends. Every single widow reported a continuing loss of friends, beginning soon after her husband's need for care became evident. In addition, some also reported an early change of friends—for example, from her friends to his.

After friends, the children went.

"I used to send Fran to, uhh, uhh, my aunt for the whole summer—you know, so that for three months she has a very peaceful (laughs) life and, uhh, Freddie used to go over to my mother - in - law's for the summer, you know, and I really couldn't afford it but I, you know, saved every penny that I could so that they could go. And, you know, I figured, well, three months out of the—out of the year——was sort of a compensation, you know (laugh)." (BANKS 8.IV.14)

The children loved it elsewhere. There was only one problem: at least one of them had difficulty in readjusting to what Mrs. Banks herself described as a "sick, sick atmosphere."

And then what would happen when they came back at the end of the summer?

"Well, Fran would just be miserable. Freddie would come back and tell all the kids what he did, you know, and all the fun that he had. But Fran—would be very depressed for a good six weeks. . . . She didn't——she

didn't want to come out of her room, out of the room."
(BANKS 8.iv.15)

Of the eight who had children, all forced special arrangements upon them because of their husbands, even
while recognizing that this was "unfair" because they, unlike their children, had a choice. They made them keep
quiet to preserve the silence, told them not to take any
problems to their fathers, had them help drag "the drunk"
into his room. Three of the eight mothers said they felt
that by these actions their chidren came to have less respect for them. Nevertheless, they continued to sacrifice.

Mrs. Grenon related a most unpleasant experience at a
football game in which her son was playing. She and her
husband had their son's girl with them; it was a rainy day
so they had to drive. She told her husband that he was absolutely not to drink, and he promised not to. She checked
his things before they went, and there was no bottle.
However, once at the game, he managed to sneak out several times, buying and downing a bottle of liquor, and becoming drunk and obnoxious. "He started on a drunk like
there was no tomorrow." Their son made a poor play and
was benched by the coach. "Of course I was suffering for
him, suffering for my husband, suffering for the team—I
suffered for everybody (laughs)! Father went up behind
the bench and swore and yelled at our son for his mistake.
By the end of the game I was really frightened." Her husband started driving, even though drunk, and Mrs. Grenon
asked if he would pull over to the curb, which he did. She
told him quietly that he had had a little too much to drink
and asked if she or their son could please drive. "He went
into a rage" and the upshot was that he drove off, leaving
all three of them on the rainy highway miles from nowhere. He did not return, and they had to hitch a ride.
Mrs. Grenon said she was surprised that he had made it

home, drunk as he was: "I hoped he had gone right over a cliff. . . . If he had shot himself right then I wouldn't have cared" (GRENON 4.III.3).

Although all of the women sacrificed for their husbands, the wives of the alcoholics were especially impoverished.

"Thanksgiving it starting to get cold; it was time to put the storm windows. My husband was supposed to put them in that day. I was just starting, I didn't even know I was pregnant because I was just a couple of months. So, he didn't—his brother came and they want some drink and he forget all about it and didn't put the window. Come Saturday, I said, 'Well he was supposed——and he wasn't working but he went out and he didn't come back, so I start to put the window in, and my son, my little boy help me. . . . I think it was too heavy for me. . . . [Mr. Morneau returned late the next day but neither said anything about it.]

"So——that was just, uhh, three weeks before Christmas and, uhh, I went to confession the day before Christmas with my son and when I came back that's when I had my miscarriage. I was trying to put my Christmas tree and I couldn't. . . . And I was trying, I had made all this, you know, fixed all the gifts and everything for the grandmother and everything, all the packages, and I, I was doing a lot of sewing at the time, and I was trying to save, you know, buying material and make little bathrobes for the boys and——pack everything, and he didn't want to put no Christmas tree. And I was after him; the kids wanted a Christmas tree. . . . Finally, God helped me, I finished with the trim on my Christmas tree, put all the packages but then it was the end, and then I lay down on that studio couch and the doctor. . . . He went next door and the woman came and she call her own doctor . . . He didn't even call for the ambulance; he run outside fast as he could put the heat in his car and he said, 'Have her ready.' They put my slippers and bathrobe and they put my coat on top of that and they carried me to his car and he brought me to the hospital right away, and they give me blood, you know, because I was hemorrhaging. And I almost passed that time."

Whether putting up the storm windows in fact caused her miscarriage, Mrs. Morneau certainly thought so. And so what does this God - fearing fervent Catholic plead for as she lies "near death"?

"But I have, I have offer my life that night, I never told; I never told them but I offer my life so that he could come back and take care of the children. But God didn't came, didn't get me but almost, almost I pass this time. I really did."

. . . you offered your life——?

"(Interrupts) When I, I saw that he wasn't coming back that night, I said, 'God, please have him back—the children need him—take me but have him back, the children need him.' " (MORNEAU 14.VIII.13–15)

Mr. Miller was the suspected malingerer whose "accident" permanently disabled him. Even though they only had welfare checks to live on he did not want his wife to go to work; when she first took a job, he placed calls to her constantly, hanging up when she came to the telephone. She ended this one day when she hung up, got into a cab, and went home. There she informed her husband that he could call her if he wished to talk with her but that he was never again to humiliate and embarrass her. She then got back into the cab and returned to work.

Mr. Miller stayed home but did virtually nothing except drink and become violent, physically as well as verbally. On several different occasions, mother and children dragged him to his room after he had passed out. At other times they called in the police, only to drop the charges the next day. There were other ways also in which they sacrificed themselves and their home to him. "The kids were getting disgusted. They hated to come home. So did I."

The four wives of alcoholics sacrificed even their own emotional stability at times.

". . . when I had the responsibility of him, and his drinking and his mental illness and the rest of it, I just—this was—I would end up in bed. I just couldn't face it. I just couldn't stand it, and, so, uhmm . . ." (GRENON 11.VIII.30)

Mrs. Banks, Grenon, Miller, and Morneau follow a closely similar pattern. Examples of losing friends, shameful episodes, family sacrifice, and emotional trauma can be heard from any one of them. The pattern extends through the hurt these four men inflicted upon their wives.

In one of the most callous of such episodes, Mr. Morneau got drunk after they had rushed to Mrs. Morneau's sister's deathbed. He went out that night with another woman, and then for the first time ever told her of it the next day while she was in mourning. Perhaps the reader will agree with her that:

"He didn't have to tell me that. I would never hear about it if he didn't told me; that hurt me. You know, I know even if he, if you have a feeling that he go out with somebody else and have a good time—if he didn't tell me I wouldn't know it." (MORNEAU 6.III.42)

The wives of the four alcoholics are also the only ones who took much personal abuse. The other eight husbands may have made other unreasonable demands on their wives, but being a "whipping boy" was not among them. For just these four, then, their hell hurt so much that they began to wonder why they took it.

Why do you think you're neurotic?

"My girlfriend told me I was (laughs)."

Just recently?

"No. No, a long time. Well, I don't know if she was serious. I think she was though. I called her up one night and I was very depressed about George. And I was talking about George and he was out like a light. Sitting right there on the couch and he couldn't hear. And I said 'I don't know why I, really! And she said, 'You're a fool, I told you you're a fool to stay there with that man. There's always a way out. The only thing that I can say is that you must get a certain amount of satisfaction out of it.' And I said, 'Are you crazy,' I said, 'You make me sound like I'm a neurotic' and she said, 'Well you are.' I said, 'I am?' She said, 'You certainly are. You've got to be to put up with a situation like that all these years.' "

And is that what made you start thinking in terms of getting out? Was that around that time?

"Not quite, it was a little, quite a bit later."

And how do you feel about that outlook? Do you think there is anything to it?

"No, not really. No I don't think so." (Banks 10.v.24)

*What do they [other friends] mean by it [neurotic] be-
cause I didn't understand what they*——

"——Well, I, I, I never could understand what they
meant by that myself. Uh, I suppose inflicting punishment
on myself. For what reason I don't know, 'cuz you know,
I've never done anything that terrible." (BANKS 15.IX.17)

Mrs. Banks may have felt that she never had done anything "that terrible" to deserve the punishment she got, but
she and the three other wives of alcoholics did continue to
allow themselves and their children to be punished. With
the four cases of wives of alcoholics, and, adding at this
point Mrs. Ago and Mrs. Jefferson whose cases are parallel
but of much shorter duration, sacrifice was demanded by
the six husbands and the wives gave it.

Mrs. Ago told of how agonizing it was for her husband
to be hooked. He had signed himself into Bridgewater
shortly before they were married 'to take the cure.' However, shortly after their marriage, he found himself fully
addicted again. She described how he resorted to pushing
the heroin and she felt that this was the most honest way
that he could make the money he needed to sustain his
habit. When he needed additional money, he would rob
places and steal cars. When asked how she felt about this
and if she knew that he was doing this, she said that she did
know and that she hated his doing it. "But when you're
hooked, your hooked body has to have that stuff because
it's so awful when you get sick and you shake and he had
to get the money somehow." She said that she had only the
dimmest future to look forward to and tried not to look
beyond the next day. She knew that it could only end
badly, but didn't know that it would end in death (AGO
4.I.8).

For the six silent caretakers the price of caring included,
as we have heard, sacrifice and personal abuse. The take-

over managers also paid a high price for their caretaking, but it rarely included personal abuse. Rather, the demands made upon them were in the nature of additional strength and new abilities—for example, Mrs. Burke, who said she had to become a different person. Mrs. Sullivan and Mrs. Tibbetts found they had to care for their husbands as for their children. Instead of watching a regular loss of friends, family, and material resources, the loss they experienced was born of the care they had to give.

"I have always protected Doc from any problems that were in the house; I would kill the kids if they said anything in front of their father that would make him upset and get him into a mood for weeks at a time. I have always shielded Doc in that line; I've always taken care of all the problems myself or the children's since Doc has been sick." (SULLIVAN 3.11.37)

"I protected Father, if the kids did something and Father found out about it, then for four or five days he would get very—course to me it was moods, but I learned afterwards that it was depression. I called them Father's 'moods'—he wouldn't talk to anybody for four or five days. So I found out that if he didn't know what the kids were doing, then he wouldn't get in those moods. So I wouldn't let the kids talk about anything that would upset Father, in that way. . . . I didn't baby him, I protected him from getting into his moods. 'Cuz I would have to live with Father when he was in those depressions. . . . after he got sick, then he would complain about he was no good to himself, he was no good to me, he was no good to the children. 'Cuz he was no longer a man. And you'd listen to that for three or four days, you would get——there was one time there I used to be so sick of people bein' sick that my kids would come in and say they were sick and I would say, 'Don't bother me, go tell your Father.' I just hated people to be sick around me. I suppose where Father was sick for so long and he'd get into those awful moods of his, and wouldn't talk to anybody, and wouldn't get out of bed, wouldn't get out of the chair. And after a while—you can only feel sorry for so long—then after a while you get mad." (SULLIVAN 5.IV.22–23)

"You can only feel sorry for so long," Mrs. Sullivan states, after she managed her husband's problems for more than twenty years. She did get mad—refused to do any grocery shopping unless he took her, which he finally did—yet on the more important issues like finding some work he could do at home, or allowing her to work, she told us of no protest. She even found out about and prepared all the papers for the compensation he was eligible to receive as well as the veterans' payments.

Gradually, if not from the outset, these six women took over. Three earned the income necessary for support; among those not working, two did not need the money and one was not permitted to work by her husband. When more money was needed, Mrs. Zack took on a second job; Mrs. Sullivan asked her relatives. Five of the six handled the money, and the five who had children raised them by their own rules, even when it meant giving a child to the husband to manage.

While the silent caregivers took much personal abuse and suffered many losses, those who took over followed a different pattern. Increasingly they found themselves playing what we have referred to as the mutual deception game. Mrs. Sullivan has already called it "protecting Father from his moods"; Mrs. Sloat called it "keeping Tommy from getting hurt." By any name it meant first screening the husband from the outside world, and then screening the outside world from him. These women put a good face on anything they possibly could, hoping by that action to make things better. It was not that they pretended that everything was all right while doing nothing about it. They all knew the nature of the problem better than anyone else, and benevolently controlled information into and out of their husband's lives; all, that is, except Mrs. Zack, who was too bitter for benevolence. Their deception varied by degree of kin and type of relationship, yet they all practiced it. There were some things he would not be told—and some things that he later would not tell them.

THE DOWNWARD SPIRAL

"I knew the only way I could go with him was down," Mrs. Banks stated, and that is just where each one of our twelve women was now headed. It did not matter whether they were silent or domineering caregivers, for the husbands of both types continued to deteriorate. The prematurely aged Mr. Tibbetts had to seek medical retirement from the state and quit work. For different reasons but with the same effect, Mr. Sloat and Mr. Banks could find no new employer and so they sank a little further down. With the possible exceptions of Mrs. Codman and Mrs. Zack, these women were all headed down without seeking any outside help to reverse their descent.

Can you go to AA yourself as the wife, even if the husband isn't interested in going? Can you go to AA to get information about how to handle it or how to help?

"Yes, you can."

Did you ever try anything like that?

"No, uh - uh. No, I never tried it. Because he said he was never an alcoholic, so, he wasn't an alcoholic."

Of course you knew he was and you were dealing with this problem. And did you feel that AA couldn't help you, or was there some other reason that you didn't go, to somebody like that?

"No, because George was a rebel, and from the very beginning, he just wouldn't go for something like that." (BANKS 10.v.39)

Even with such forceful interviewing the question "Why didn't you get help?" goes unanswered. When their husbands did seek help from some experienced organization, at best the wives merely went along.

Did you ever ask anybody at AA what to do or if you should talk to him when he was sober or, you know, did they give you any advice of what to do?

"No, because, uhh, in AA, when he was in AA, everybody feel that he was doing wonderful and me, I know he wasn't doing that but I just didn't want to go against them. You know what I——"

Oh, so you didn't tell them?

"No. No, no, no, no, I never—NEVER to do anything, you know, to try to be, uhh, opposite to him. You know, I always say like him. Maybe that was the trouble, at first, you know if I had tried at first before he get too far gone, maybe——he wouldn't be that way. But, uh, I never wanted to." (MORNEAU 4.ii.33)

Men who need care and women who with equal intensity needed to care—this is one theme that resonates throughout our widows' narratives. Coupled with that is the observation that they alone were to be the caregivers, for most sought no help for their husbands, although some sought it for themselves.

"I was really falling to pieces myself. I, I had become so nervous that I couldn't, I couldn't go into stores, I couldn't sit in church, I couldn't walk on the street, I was going to psychiatrists and doctors and just about anybody that would talk to me to find out what was wrong with me. I was crying all the time, and well, it was just terrible. It, it was, uh, well the psychiatrist up at the up, Brigham Hospital said to me that, you know, that I was just so insecure and anxious, and uh, he didn't help me very much up there. He said, 'Go home and stop eating.' That's what he told me to do. I was eating myself to death. I was one seventy - four at that point and then I went to another psychiatrist and he was trying to help me but by that time my husband had a nervous breakdown, so that broke up my help with that psychiatrist. But it was just——you know, one doctor right after another trying to keep myself going. I think the best thing I ever did was go to work." (GRENON 9.VII.24)

"He kept having his way," these widows told us, even when his way threatened quite literally to destroy them in the process. Mrs. Jefferson convincingly related two incidents where her husband tried to kill her, first with gas while she was sleeping one night, and then later with a knife. How did these women manage to carry on?

"In the back of my mind I'd say, oh well, you know, things are gonna get better. Like when the kids were small, you know, I'd say, well things are gonna get better. The kids are gonna get bigger and they'll be on their own and then I'll be able to do this, and I'll be able to do that. Well the kids did get bigger; they did get on their own, but I was still there." (BANKS 8.IV.25)

They were still there, telling themselves that things would get better, that at least they still had a roof over their heads and food on the table. They told themselves whatever was necessary so that they could continue to give whatever their husbands seemed to need from them.

"I'd come home. Well, some times I didn't but most of the times I did. And when I came home, by the time I did, eleven, eleven - thirty, he'd be out like a light, which was good because it meant I got some sleep. Otherwise he'd just keep me up all night. I mean, I went through that so many times. I couldn't even count the times I went through that. As a matter of fact now, I would never go through that, but as a matter of fact now, I don't know how I managed to keep my sanity." (BANKS 10.V.23)

During their married lives their husbands would threaten the sanity of Mrs. Banks, Codman, and Grenon, the life of Mrs. Jefferson, and at the least the home and family of Mrs. Ago, Miller, and Morneau. Yet these women continued to give care. And their husbands continued to deteriorate.

Silence as well as deception distorts communication, and the thrust of this process is clearly revealed in the way in which they responded to their husbands' attempts to commit suicide. Only one of the six wives whose husbands attempted suicide confronted him with it.

Did you talk to him about the attempt, asking him why he did it?

"No. I was—no, at that point, umm, it was sort of a big nightmare to me. I, I took to my bed and (laughs) when he was up in the hospital I was so shaken by the whole thing, uhmm, I felt guilty myself; I thought I had done it, you know, because you know if I had been a good wife this could never have happened, and uhmm, like—— because the doctor said to me, upon leaving now, 'Talk to your husband, talk to your husband. When he comes home at night, talk to him.' He was——and I would say to him, 'I can't talk with him; he won't talk with me.' 'Well you know, he's got to for his mental health.' Well it's one thing to say that and another to do it (laughs)."

Right. If someone doesn't want to talk there isn't very much you can do.

"Right. No. No, you can't; you can't drag it out of him and so, you see as a result I just felt more guilty and more guilty all the time. I felt well gee, if I can't talk to him, who's going to talk with him, and it's all my fault. Why won't he talk with me?"

You never did refer then to the suicide attempt?

"No, because I think I felt so guilty about the whole thing anyway that I like swept it right under the rug. I just, uhh, I felt we won't talk about it; we won't, uhm, dwell on it; we'll just pretend that everything's all fine now and . . ." (GRENON 6.v.30)

Mrs. Grenon is of the coexisting, silent management pattern, as are Mrs. Miller, Morneau, and Jefferson, all of whose husbands attempted suicide and none of whom talked to their husbands about it. Although Mrs. Codman "took over" her husband, she did not discuss his attempt with him either.

Did you ever talk to him about his suicide attempt when you were on your way to visit him in Wisconsin?

"——You know, I'm trying to recall back.——I can't remember discussing it with him at that time. We did discuss it later on.——I really can't recall discussing it with him at that time.——It seems ridiculous when you think about it——How do you ignore something like that? But I can't remember going——and I'm sure if we had gone into any deep discussions about it, uh, I would recall. There might have been a feeling that the obvious is the obvious. Uh, and uh, you know (laughs)." (CODMAN 14.viii.20)

Alone among the six wives whose husbands attempted suicide, Mrs. Sloat—of the twelve the woman with the least education—responded immediately and sensibly.

"Oh, the night after it happened, on a Sunday night, Monday morning I went to work, and of all the crazy things for me to do was to go to my boss and tell her. So the next day was a holiday, and I didn't want to lose the holiday pay, so I went to the boss and I said, 'Mary, my husband tried to commit suicide last night.' She said 'Go home now, go home'—she acted real quick. Instead of going home, I went to my mother - in - law's first. And my mother - in - law said 'Well, what is the cause of this?' I said 'I don't know, I haven't talked to Tommy yet.' I said 'He was sleeping when I left for work this morning, and I hope he's still sleeping now.' She said 'I'll go with you.' I said 'I hope we get there before he wakes up.' When we got there he was still in bed, and when he knew his mother was there he hid his face underneath the blankets, he didn't want to see his mother. He said to me, 'You had to go get my mother?' I said 'Look, I had to let your mother know what happened because if she hears about this, it's gonna be rougher on both of us.' I said 'She's gotta know. She's your mother.' So she talked to him, he told her he was happy about the baby and happy about being married, it was just that he was down because he wasn't working.

"I took him to the hospital—they wanted to put him in a mental—I didn't want them to—if they were I was going to walk out on them, 'cuz I knew he wasn't crazy, and that it was a matter of a slight depression. And I was thinkin' of him being so young—why should he be grounded for life with the thing over him of that? That would be the worst thing I could do. And I told the doctor and he said, 'Well, if you don't do this you'll be held responsible,' and I said, 'Well, he ain't gonna do anything.' He sez, 'Well, if he goes home tonight and jumps out the window—you're to blame.' But he gave him medication and he slept the whole night." (SLOAT 12.VI.20–22)

Six of the husbands attempted suicide; four of them were married to the silent management type, and their wives responded to their attempts with additional silence. Of the other two, only one of the attempted suicides discussed his attempt with his wife.

The need for care and the need to care now enfolded both conjugants in a net from which neither saw any escape. The silence of the past, which had failed to change the course of their lives, gave rise to additional silence, even in the sight of suicide itself. Management through domination also remained unchanged, even when the attempt at suicide discredited it. Only the cost of caring changed, as it now began to rob even the marital bed.

Although our information about the sexual lives of the twelve couples is scanty, what is available sheds additional light on our research volunteers' lives.

What about the sexual part of the relationship? Was that affected too?

"Yeah, I guess, to some degree. Uh - hum. We still, you know, went to bed together but it wasn't, uh, as enjoyable for me. You know, it became more of a, uh, you know, a routine, gee, it's the night again, sort of thing. You know, uh, oh, I think that was probably one of the last things to deteriorate. Um, but, um——" (ZACK 9.III.11)

For the young student-wife Mrs. Zack, although sex was the last thing to deteriorate, it finally went as well. With the other young wife, Mrs. Jefferson, it went like this.

"Phil, I had to teach him. Phil had never bothered with women before."

He was a virgin, was he?

"Yes, and uh (laughs)." *How interesting!* "It somewhat —I dug on it, you know, because he was so pure sort of, and it was barbaric (laughter). It was more like getting raped than it was, than it was——(laughing) and I sort of thought, yeah, but after a while it nauseated me."

Well, did he ever get good at it?

"No, he was so uncoordinated. There wasn't any—it really wasn't anything."

Couldn't you teach him to get——?

"No, I tried (laughs)."

How soon after you knew him did it get rather bad?

"Uhh, a couple of weeks. Yah, before I married him."
(JEFFERSON 8.VI.14)

Mrs. Ago and Mrs. Sloat, the other two women under
thirty, did not give us information about their sex lives.
For the three women in their forties, sex was discussed and
proved to be at least a physical problem. It was a problem
for the Codmans because of his paralysis. For the Tibbetts,
it was a procreative problem: ". . . I had said, 'Gee,
wouldn't it be nice if we had a little girl?' And he almost
passed out, but uh, but, you know, uh, with his tuberculosis and with his X rays, I think this is what made him sterile. And we couldn't have any kids" (TIBBETTS 9.VIII.10).
And for the third woman in her forties, sex was just a
problem.

"We really didn't have sexual compatibility for a good
many years because—we did when we were first
married—very happy for awhile—but my husband
with sex, as well as with everything else that he did—
this was a time that he really needed to be bolstered with
liquor too. And he never really made love to me when he
was sober. For a while I thought that this was the way that
life was, you know. Then I revolted against it—then I
was revolted by it. Then I plain just wouldn't have anything to do with him. Except for periods when I would
think to myself that it was all my fault—he told me I
was cold—a very cold woman. I was convinced of this
too. Until I went to the psychiatrist, then I realized that it
wasn't all my fault, because he turned me off." (GRENON
4.III.16)

Among the other five women, all of whom were over fifty years of age when we interviewed them, Mrs. Sullivan reported sexual activity until the last four years or so.

"Well, I don't think I kissed Father in what, four years. Because he said there was no sense to it (laughs). He, he didn't, if he got affectionate, you know, there was no sense to it. It didn't, it wouldn't go anywhere, so don't bother him." (SULLIVAN 4.III.6)

Somewhat of a pattern seemed to emerge when Mrs. Miller reported:

"Well I don't know, I was never highly sexed. I often wondered why I—how come I ever had children (laughs), as a matter of fact. Uh, never, very seldom, did I enjoy sex.——It's an awful thing to say, but it's true."

So, how did you feel about it most of the time when you knew that you were going to have sex every night?

"I didn't like it ever. Usually, he'd tell me I was cold. ——Which I couldn't help. I didn't mean to be; but that's the way I was." (MILLER 11.VI.54)

Mrs. Burke volunteered no information and Mrs. Morneau stated that although she later found out differently, while married she never refused because she thought "in my religion you're not supposed to refuse a man." That leaves Mrs. Banks.

Was he impotent in the last while?

"Yah."

He had interest in sex, did he?

"Oh, yah, he had an interest—he did have an interest, but, but, uh, you know—with all the drinking that he did, he was killing it more, and that's what it was; but I would tell him that, you know. I told him the reason for it. Well——I'd say about five years, you know, before his death, I used to tell him, you know, that, and he used to say. . . . 'No, no,' you know, and he would give me one excuse after another, you know, the reason that he couldn't and uhh—he would tell me the reason that he couldn't—because he knew that I didn't love him. Well that's, you know, we know—like (laughs) that's not true. But he just never would, you know, face the fact that it was drinking. I'd tell him, I'd say, 'It's your drink.' I said, 'I bet if you stayed away from drinking for three months, you wouldn't have any problem whatsoever.' Now, IF ——I was AFTER him——for sex, you see, then I could understand, you know, this attitude, but I wasn't. The only time, you know, that I would bring it up was when he would say, you know, 'Well I don't get any sex from you'; then I would have to, you know——have to justify myself. 'You don't get any sex from me because, you know, you can't, uhh——you just can't come up with it any more. That's all.' And that was the truth. He, he just couldn't. And anyway, you know, he would keep me awake all night, which was, uhh——nervewracking, to say the least. I mean——"

You mean trying to be successful at it?

"Yeah, trying to be. But I was—three, four o'clock in the morning and I had to get up at seven o'clock to go to work——things like that." (BANKS 12.VII.28)

Interestingly, three of the four wives of alcoholics said that their husbands said they were "cold." We know little about the kind of sex life they and the others had earlier, but we do know that conjugal sex relations were virtually nonexistent toward the end. Perhaps when that basic relationship deteriorated it accompanied if not precipitated the collapse of the entire marital relationship.

THREE WAYS OF DYING

THE TWELVE CONJUGAL PAIRS had enough in common to allow us to tell their story together thus far. There was a more or less usual childhood in seemingly ordinary families, marriage to men who needed care and then more care, and the bond of the spouses in their need to have care and the equally strong need to give care. There followed the intensification of the conjugal relationship based on care until it organized all of the life space.

Did you and your family ever go on vacations or any place during the summer time?

"No, I like to sleep in my own bed. I don't like, uhh, no, really with Father the way he was, you couldn't, uhh, travel or any place like that because, uhh, he wanted his

own house and his own bed and——we'd go down
Henry's for cookouts and stuff like that on weekends, but
he didn't like going away. When somebody's sick like that,
well you just run your life to that way." (SULLIVAN
3.II.29–30)

From birth to marriage through the downward spiral of
life before death the twelve women display common patterns. All twelve women continued to live with their husbands up until now. They threatened, they complained,
and they suffered, but they slept in the same house and
usually in the same bed. They lost their friends, their
neighbors, their families, their children, their financial and
emotional resources, and still they continued the care.

Something then happened to cause seven of them to reverse this enduring pattern; they broke from their conjugants. The story of these seven pairs is told in the following section, "The Socially Dying."

While these seven began to experience loss by social
death at this point in their lives, two other pairs began to
prepare for the natural death they expected. Doc Sullivan
as well as Don Burke began to physically die, and so their
wives expected death but not suicide. Their story is told in
the section entitled "The Physically Dying."

Only three conjugal pairs were "Strangers to Death,"
and their story is told in this third and final section.

All three of these sections carry the story through the
end of our field work, which was usually fifteen months
after the physical death of the husband.

THE SOCIALLY DYING

Two years before his physical death, Mr. Miller began to
die socially from the life of his wife and five children. First,

Mrs. Miller legally separated from him, then she secured a court order to keep him away, and finally she had him committed to a state mental hospital for six months. Although the other six widows in this group of seven broke with their husbands in less drastic ways, their experiences followed a similar pattern: The lives of care that we observed earlier were reversed.

Of the four that decided to separate, Mrs. Miller and Mrs. Zack forced their husbands out, and Mrs. Grenon and Mrs. Banks left themselves. The three other wives continued to reside with their husbands; two of them, however, spent periods of time elsewhere, and the third began to withdraw from emotional relations. These ruptures in the conjugal relationship were the beginning of the "death" of each for the other.

"When we came home that night I said, 'Lester I want a divorce. I'd just had it. . . . It took me a long time to decide it, but when I had had it, I'd had it. You know, I mean, that was it." (ZACK 9.III.13–14)

"I was just adamant about this . . . 'I want a divorce. That's all there is to it. I'm not wasting any more time' . . . My mind was made up, I wanted a divorce and as far as I was concerned, I didn't want to see him the rest of my life. You know. Except in court, and that was it." (ZACK 12.v.16)

To wish not to see a person the rest of his life is to will the end of his life with you. Regardless of what other life he might lead, this one was finished, dead. It represented not just the death of a relationship, but also the death of what they had been to each other.

Life for all of us is a series of such deaths, the discarding of old selves we no longer wish to be. Each such transition has its own cycle of withdrawal from one self and integration into another, its own rhythm of death and rebirth. The physical death of a spouse is the loss of a love, but so is separation. What difference does it make if the person lives, but elsewhere, when he has already died in the life of his spouse? The relationship, what one person was to another, has ended, and perhaps only slightly less than when physical death is involved.

People live for us while we live with them; when life in common ends, the person has in effect died. Thus death for these seven women began with the end of their lives with their husbands. Mrs. Miller, Banks, Zack, and Grenon stopped living with their husbands. Mrs. Banks kept her new address and telephone number a closely guarded secret to insure her break with George. She began to go out with other men, as did Mrs. Grenon and Mrs. Zack.

The fifth woman who began to end her life with her husband was Mrs. Morneau. She almost forcibly institutionalized him, and when he returned home she maintained extreme emotional distance. "He had done too much and my heart was hard like a rock." Mrs. Jefferson also still resided with her husband at the time of his death, but she had not spent the previous night with him and in other ways was beginning to disengage herself.

Mrs. Codman, the seventh woman well into preparation for life without her husband, began to distance herself after he had begged her to kill him. He had secured a pistol for that purpose, and had attempted to press it upon her that night. Later she learned through an associate that he had purchased some poison, so she expected his suicide at any moment.

These seven widows thus stood at different points in their withdrawal from their husbands, from Mrs. Miller's almost completely rebuilt life, to Mrs. Codman's anticipatory one. They all essentially conform to a common pattern in their approach to the death of their husbands. Since we need to examine their lives in considerable detail to observe this pattern, we will follow only a single case, that of Mrs. Banks.

First, there was a period of living with the other, and yet feeling alone.

"Well, I'll be very honest with you——the last year or two when George and I were—uh—living together (sigh) I was pretty well on my own. I couldn't depend on him for anything. See it's not a case, you know, where your husband gets killed by an automobile or something, and, uhhh, and, you know, you have all these adjustments to go through, you know; it wasn't anything like that with me. I'd had to——I was more or less on my own for as long as two years." (BANKS 12.VII.49)

The twenty - year pattern of silence, of avoiding any problem, was then broken.

". . . I still do hold things in a long time, and then I get to the point where, you know, like it's the breaking point, you know, where the rubber band snaps and then I'd just go CRAZY, you know; and that's what I used to do with him. And, uhm, you know, I always tried to make him feel like a man, because I, you know, once you take that away from a man they really——then, you know, there's no hope for him EVER, and, uhh, I always tried to DO this to him, but, when I would GET to that point, you know, then I, I would just——explode and really tell him, you know, what my true feelings were——what he was and the way he was going, what was going to happen to him . . .

"I'd call him an alcoholic, which he always denied. Uhh——and then I, you know, would, uhhh——

would discuss facts and tell him, you know, that he was
finished, which he was . . ." (BANKS 12.VII.28)

In this way the husband learned his wife was leaving
him, although she could not actually tell him yet. She first
communicated her decision to various persons *outside* the
family.

"May, ya, the first part of May last year—and we
owed him about three months rent, and he told me, 'Well,
the only reason I'm not doing anything about it is because
of you. Otherwise you would have gotten an eviction notice a long time ago.' I said, 'Well, don't let that stop you
because I'm not going to be here much longer. You go
right ahead with it.' " (BANKS 10.V.22)

By telling her landlord to evict them, by advising her
friends that she was finally leaving George "pretty soon,"
and by telling George himself that "he was finished, which
he was," Mrs. Banks prepared herself for what she knew
she must finally do. This was *preparatory socialization*, as
it is called in sociology, referring to the social psychological processes an individual goes through in passing from
one status to another—in this case, from being married
to being separated. Although we are using only Mrs. Banks
to tell this important part of the story, it is isomorphic to
the other six when viewed as sociological process. Although they feared the bottom of the downward spiral
they had been on for so long, they still could not leave
their other half. How could they escape? Maybe, they fan-
tasized, something would happen to him.

Years ago they had hoped that things would get better,
but instead everything got worse. Now they hoped that
things would get worse.

"Well, you know, secret, well, secretly I hoped that some, that he would get, and this is an awful thing to say, but I always did, always prayed——that he would become physically ill so that he wouldn't be able to drink anymore. Like, you know, I had hoped that it would affect his kidneys, not, not bad enough .that, you know——" (BANKS 15.IX.21)

Almost as if he were reading her thoughts, Mr. Banks did in fact become worse.

"And you know he got this terrible gash in his head [from a brawl] and he was really a mess. And that didn't shake him up at all! He got worse as a matter of fact. And I knew there was no hope for him at all. THE ONLY WAY I COULD GO IF I STAYED WITH HIM WAS DOWN." (BANKS 10.V.26)

A timeless lesson of sociology has it that we do, in fact, behave largely in terms of others' expectations of us: we are a good boy for our mother, a brave soldier for our commander, a responsible father for our children. What is often overlooked is another type of such expectations: to be queer to the straight, sick to the doctor, hateful to the hated. Expectations can be negative as well as positive, destructive as well as constructive, evil as well as good. Only the truly saintly among us have never wished another person ill, have never expected and encouraged the worst. That we may not have been vocal about it does not matter. Human communication is not limited to spoken words, but is transmitted in many ways.

"I am going to propose that people destroy themselves in response to an invitation originating from others that he stop living . . . the invitation is extended by others, that is, originates in someone's consciousness, sometimes as a conscious wish that the person stop existing, in that way, or at all, sometimes as an unconscious wish; sometimes not so openly, but rather as an indifference to the continued existence of the person in question. In whatever mode the wish for death, or the indifference to continued existence, appears, it is communicated to the one we might call the suicide. He experiences himself as being invited to stop living, and he obliges." (JOURARD, p. 133)

Perhaps Mrs. Banks now truly became terrified as she witnessed her wish coming true. As she tells us of the period ten months later, her words begin to ring with an intensified desperation.

"I couldn't continue work. I was making more mistakes at work, that last time, that was another reason, you know I was, and my temper would flare up, you know, I'm a pretty easy-going person, but I'd get uptight, you know even my friends said, the few that knew me, said, 'You've got to get away. There's really something happening to you.' I couldn't concentrate. Really like in the morning if I were in my closet, I'd stand there for about a half an hour thinking, 'What am I going to wear?' With all my clothes there, I couldn't get myself together, I couldn't think anymore. And I knew I just HAD to get out." (BANKS 10.v.26)

Her daughter had been telling her whenever she started to complain about her husband: "Now, you know what you've got to do, so I don't want to hear it." A "very good friend," one woman at work, and her relatives had also been telling her that she should leave George. *His* aunt and uncle were reported by *her* to have said: "I don't know how you can stand it and, you know, you really should get away because, uhhh, uh——you know, you're ruining your life, your health." Mrs. Banks concluded, saying: ". . . people were just saying, were telling me that they noticed a change——they noticed a change in my looks, my attitude" (BANKS 6.III.18).

She stayed. After living alone with him; after telling him all those things she had been holding back all these years; after telling others that she was finally leaving him; after her fondest wishes that he get worse came true without improving things between them, she stayed. She then felt he threatened her.

"Finally, I mean I, last year I got my income tax check and I did manage to——you know, have some money put away. So I just—put that away. I told him I was going——I think really the thing, the thing that REALLY made me leave him was——he, uhh, he was threatening me. You know, like he'd say 'Look,' I'd say, 'Lookit, George, we can't go on like this. Now we've got to do something. You have to straighten yourself out and I'll help you, but I know that I can't do it because I've been trying for years, so you've got to get some outside help.' He'd say, 'Well, you're the one that needs it,' you know. I said, 'I probably do now after all these years of living the way we have; I know I need help. I'm willing to get it; how about you?' 'I don't need it,' he'd say, 'If you're so unhappy here, why don't you go, GO!' And he kept you know, throwing all these threats in my face . . ." (BANKS 8.IV.26)

What were these threats? Perhaps after all her sacrifice, after all her care over twenty years he could say in a rare moment of truth that he could do without her.

". . . after I was paying all the bills. Almost all the furniture that was there I had bought, and it's just that I felt like now, what is wrong with me? Am I crazy? I, you know, and, oh, what am I, I mean, you know, am I trying to——destroy myself? Am I masochist or something? I had to, you know, something's got to be wrong with me and actually I worried about myself, you know. So, and that's when I made the decision——that I HAD to leave because if I didn't, oh, I don't know where I would have been because I really don't. Because I really felt like my mind was snapping—I mean my power of concen—I couldn't concentrate; I was very short tempered, very nervous——couldn't sleep, worried——

"I was scared——I was—when I thought about it, you know, I thought about him, you know. You know——was I going to make out——and like, you know, I mean he, he was so insulting when he was drinking and then I would think about him you know, insulting somebody and maybe getting beat up and all that, you know. I felt very guilty. Although everybody says, you know, you have to be sick to feel guilty about it, but I did. And I couldn't help it, I did feel guilty.

"I knew that it was the best thing. I mean, it was the only thing. I mean I didn't have any choice. This was what I had to do——because he really got me up against the wall—really." (BANKS 8.IV.27)

"One's not half two; it's two are halves of one" * must be remembered at this point. Mrs. Banks did not single-handedly destroy her husband by wishing him ill; he did not drive her up against the wall all by himself either. He needed care and she felt the need to be needed. Care became *the* bond of their conjugality, joining both to the worst that was within them. The worse he became the

* E. E. Cummings, *Complete Poems, 1913–1962*, by permission of Harcourt Brace Jovanovich, Inc.

more she had to stay. In fact, if he would only become incapacitated, then she would really be needed. When he did, in fact, become worse yet said that he didn't need her, the bottom dropped out of her life. She knew that George had never before needed so much—he was no longer able to work and was without health, money, or any visible means of support. Mrs. Banks must have known that indeed George was finished. When he then rejected the care she still would have continued, she must have known that he was going all the way down. Just as he had seemed to read her ill wishes for him, so she must have known that he intended to die. So she *had* to stop even sharing quarters with this willing candidate for death.

Each woman had communicated to her husband an invitation to die, or at least to stop living in the way in which they had. They gave social form to that invitation by residentially and emotionally separating from their husbands at this time. By act and thought they communicated their secret feelings toward their husbands, while feeling under murderous attack from their rejection of them. It is often suggested that some suicides symbolize the murder of the surviving mate, the inward acting out of aggression felt for the other. Perhaps these women now felt within what they would soon feel from without—nothing less than a murderous attack on their very existence. On *that* Day, and on some of those that follow, more than one of these women would contemplate giving their deceased husbands their way once again.

Paths to survival must indeed be sought, even as these women sought a way out. But first they experienced even deeper difficulties. Mrs. Grenon reported that she worried more about her husband after they separated because "there was nobody to look out after him." She also left him because she felt that she was losing her mind and had no other course (3.II.37–38). Her husband had previously attempted suicide, as had Mr. Miller and Mr.

Morneau. Among all seven, however, only Mrs. Morneau actually said she had a presentiment. When, thirteen months later, she told us the following, she added that she had never told anyone before.

After the time that he tried to commit suicide, did you worry about that or watch out for it?

"No. Because I thought he was all right. You know I thought as long as——I knew he had to take some of the pills and I was, I was trying to stop him so he wouldn't take too much, but I knew he had to take it because I knew if he didn't have it, uh——something happen to him. Only the day before——it's funny——the day before I knew from the way he act, I have in my mind that he was thinking of it. I hide all the knives I have. I had hide them so he wouldn't find them. And, and I didn't think of that, but you see they, but they say you always have like a presentiment you know, when something will happen. And that's what I have the day before." (MORNEAU 13.VII.23)

Guilty knowledge was thus to be added to their burden before their husbands would put down theirs. Only old - fashioned, strong Mrs. Morneau could tell us what at least some of the others had to hide even from themselves. "Not that, too!" some of them must have felt somewhere in their minds, minds that at the moment were focused on the way out of the death plunge of their husbands.

Finally, shattering the silence, they told their husbands what they thought of them. After telling first others and then even their husbands, they fled. They fled fearing, if not their very lives, at least their sanity.

Three still resided with their husbands just before the

suicide, but for them life with their husbands had already ended.

Their Penultimate Communication

The last time Mrs. Grenon talked to her husband was at the time of their separation, not quite two months before his suicide. Mr. Banks telephoned his wife at work about two weeks before his suicide, asking her to cash in his insurance policy. She met him downtown and gave him half the five hundred dollars she had received. The Zacks also made money the basis of their last verbal exchange. He telephoned to ask if she had received his check for the money he owed her. "I remember when I hung up I thought how strange, we didn't fight."

Mr. Miller tried unsuccessfully to talk to his wife several days before his death. Mrs. Jefferson did not spend the night before with her husband. He reportedly had attacked her and she had fled to her parents' home. We have already heard from Mrs. Morneau. The Codmans had breakfast together that morning before he went to work.

THAT Day

"That day I went to work as usual. My husband went to sign his unemployment check that morning but he didn't pick it up——it came in the mail a few days later. He went . . . and bought some liquor, then he must have brought the car home because he walked to the bridge. When he got near the bridge, he met a friend who worked at the textile school, which is right near the bridge, and he asked the friend to stay with him a while. This was so unusual for my husband——he was a real loner. He would never ask for anybody to keep him company. I think he knew the pill was taking over, and he wanted to hang on to somebody to keep from doing what he had in mind. I think he took the alcohol for courage to do it. Anyway the friend said that he couldn't stay with Jim because he had some errands to do. A little while later, this friend saw Jim sitting on a step with his head in his hands. The friend went back to the school, a few minutes later looked out the window and saw a big crowd on the bridge.

"Two policemen——I didn't know they were police-men then because they were dressed in regular clothes—— came to my factory. I was called up to the office where they told me that my husband had an accident, and they wanted to take me to him at the hospital. I was dirty, and had my old shoes and apron on, but I just went upstairs and got my pocketbook and coat and went with them. When I got outside I saw the police car, and when they started to ask me about my parish priest, I thought to my-self it must be some accident if they're asking questions like that. I couldn't get up the courage to ask them more about it. When I got to the hospital, they put me in a little room and they asked me if I had children nearby. I told them about my son who works at Worthington Mills and they asked me his telephone number. I couldn't remember it and they said, 'That's okay, we'll find it out.' I waited there for more than a half hour——they were waiting for my son to come before they told me anything——and believe me, I rubbed my hands so much they weren't dirty any-more. Then they came in with my son and a nun and they told me what happened. The worst thing is they wouldn't let me see him——they wanted me to remember him as he was. I know they were trying the best for me, but I'm sorry that I listened to them on this (cries).

"If only I could have seen him. He fell on his face and it

was all smashed up and they thought I really shouldn't see him, that I would have bad memories, but if I just could have touched his foot or something, I would feel so much better. The coffin was closed too so I could never see him." (MORNEAU 2.1.12)

Mr. Zack jumped from a building. Mr. Jefferson hung himself.

"Oh, well, see I stood [stayed] here that night because Phil tried to kill me and I, uh, me and my younger sister went home, uh, my home where he was, figuring— because I didn't think he could get in and she was my security sort of, like if he tried to kill me she could run for help (laughs) and, uh, he had got into the apartment and up until now I still don't know how; both doors were locked and he didn't have a key, and he had the door barricaded and I couldn't get in. So I went back here and I knew something happened, you know, even my mother knew. You could just tell and the next morning I didn't want to go home, you know, I didn't want to go home, I kept hestitating here and that afternoon, you know, I had to go home sooner or later, and I knew I was gonna find him dead. And my mother and sister waited downstairs in the car and I went up and there was a note on the front door saying, 'Cathy I love you. You're right, I am crazy —blah, blah, blah—and thank you for trying to love me. Phil.' Then I walk in the door and the place is a shamble and I had just cleaned it the day before, and umm, there were sort of a hall, no not a hall, a sort of opening through the rooms like where the doors were and I see him hanging on the bathroom door and, you know, I thought he was faking because he, he heard me coming. So—this was typical of him (laughs) so I walk up to him and I start shaking him and you could just feel it, you know, and,

and, I was sort of shocked off and backed off and just stood there looking at him. So I went to the window and I called my sister up and she gets out of the car smiling. She thought I was fooling you know, I wanted to punched the window out telling her to hurry, and, uh, she comes running up the steps and she starts screaming and yelling and I, I didn't cry; I couldn't. Yeah, and then my mother came up and you should have heard her scream and they went downstairs and called the cops and (laughs) I was still there looking at him, and then they dragged me downstairs, you know, and I just sat in a chair and smoked cigarettes." (JEFFERSON 6.III.43–46)

Mrs. Grenon hadn't heard anything from her husband for several weeks. Then his boss of many years called to ask if she knew where he was. She told him of their separation and gave him her husband's new address. He went to Jack's apartment, perhaps to fire him, then called Mrs. Grenon and the police.

What did he say when he called?

"Well, he could hardly speak, because you can imagine walking into a, you know, a thing like that was pretty, pretty bad, and——he said that, he said, 'I've just found the most terrible thing. I can't even tell you.' He could hardly, you know, talk about it, and he said, 'Jack's gone. And I said, 'Where has he gone?' And he said, 'Well' —— he didn't say he'd killed himself, he said, 'He's dead.' But he didn't say that he'd killed himself. He said, 'He's DEAD' and that's all he said. And, then, uhm, you know I was so shocked that he was dead, I never thought to ask him HOW he had died; I thought he probably had a heart attack or had taken some pills, or something like

that——because he had tried to kill himself once before
. . ." (GRENON 11.VIII.6)

After thus breaking the news, no one would tell Mrs.
Grenon that her husband had shot himself. Not until
twelve hours later when Jack's boss called her again was she
finally informed.

Of these four deaths thus far, all were violent and obviously suicides. Mr. Codman's mode of suicide is tradi-
tionally considered nonviolent, but was also obviously suicide. He went into his office, dictated some letters and
some other material, "and I can hear his voice [from the
tapes he dictated]; I listen to his voice and it sounds perfectly normal." Then his assistant went out to get something and when he came back "twenty minutes later he
found him. He had taken cyanide." He called Mrs. Codman immediately "in panic." She went to the office after
notifying her lawyer.

Mr. Miller was living with the landlord of the building
where the rest of the Miller family lived. "He had a habit
of leaving horrible notes around the house."

And so on this Sunday, he'd left some more notes?

"Yah."

The children saw him when they came home?

"So they thought they was the same . . . until, uhh,
one——they happened to go downstairs and they saw
one to the landlord and the hall door was open, and then,
they did call to him [Mr. Miller] but they got no answer.
Then they knocked on the landlord's door and, uh,
showed him the note. They couldn't figure out what on

earth it was. So, 'What the heck is this?' All those notes at the back door, the front door, (not clear). He was sitting on the chair in the kitchen. So then they called me at work and she told me, she said to me, 'We can't wake him up.' "

The landlord tried to wake him?

"Yah."

Not the kids?

"Oh, the kids wouldn't go near him. No. So she [land-lady] said, 'What should I do? We were going to call the police but I thought I'd ask you first.' 'Well,' I said, 'you know, I can't call the police on him now,' I said, I got a re-straining order on him. . . ." So I said, 'It's up to you. You were the one that took him back. [In their custody; they took him out of the hospital where the court had sent him.] So she——I said, 'Well, if you can't wake him up,' I said. They said, 'It can't be from liquor; I don't see any bottles around but there's pills,' she said, 'on the table and a glass of water.' And I said, 'If you feel that way, if I were you I would call the police.' So, then I didn't know whether to go home; I didn't know what to do. I called the kids. And I told the kids about it. So the kids said, 'Well, we're going out.' So I said, 'If you're going out I'm not going home until I find out what's wrong. Because I thought he might just be drunk. You know, the police might revive him and he might get, you know, lose his head and try to get upstairs or something. So anyways, I called the landlady. She told me they'd taken him to the City [hospital]. . . . So I called City and they told me he was on the DL [Danger List]. . . .

"I came home and I discovered (not clear)—so my friend next door, he was a policeman, and I called him and

I asked him what I should do. So he says, 'Let me go up and see the note first.' He read the notes, and he says, 'You know, I think the doctor at City really should see these.' He said, 'Do you want us to take a ride down?' So I did go down and they were very glad because they knew nothing at City. They knew nothing at all." (MILLER 9.v.51)

Mrs. Miller feels he must have been very depressed because of the divorce action, the restraining order, and the landlord's request that he leave. Yet a note on the table listed the quantity and type of pills he had taken. The notes on the stairs were disjointed, but expressed the hope that Mrs. Miller would "take me back if I come through this." These facts, combined with the information that he had left all windows and doors open, convinced Mrs. Miller that he had not meant the suicide to be successful. (MILLER 4.II.9).

These six deaths were so obviously suicides that both death and the label of suicide were communicated simultaneously, even to Mrs. Grenon. Not so in the seventh and final case.

A friend called Mrs. Banks to tell her that while she wasn't positive, she thought she had heard on the seven-thirty morning news that Mr. Banks had been killed by a subway train during the night.

". . . I said, 'Oh, no.' . . . I said—and, and, I remember waiting through that half hour. I went—I got, uhh, dysentery in that half hour—YOU COULDN'T believe—waiting for that eight o'clock news to come on. I kept running to the bathroom every minute and HOPING, and uh, praying that it wasn't him. At eight o'clock—I knew that it was him."

What did the news report say?

"Well, just that a, uhhh————a, uh, man that was killed on the MTA, uh, was killed BY the MTA. The man couldn't ho—uh, couldn't step on his brakes and he was, uh, on the track and, uhhh——his age . . . and, uh his last known address . . . and that was it."

So at that moment you knew?

"I knew."

In that half hour, did you call anybody or do anything?

"Oh, I called Fran."

And what did she say?

"She said, 'I'll put the radio on, it can't be. It can't be.' And I guess we both—we were both listening for it at first. She heard it and then she called me and she says, uhh, 'You know, get some things on and I'll come over and I'll get ya." And that's what she did. Then I went over to, uhh, Freddie's uhhh, my son's—and, uhh——well, he was in a state of shock too." (BANKS 12.VII.23–24)

No one considered this death to be suicide, partly because of the news report, partly because in Boston all subway trains stop running at midnight. George Banks was seen walking along the subway tracks after midnight.

"I don't think that he meant to commit suicide at all. He was an alcoholic—and I think he was drunk and that he somehow thought the last train was gone. My husband could do kooky things like that when he was drunk." (BANKS 2.I.3)

The condition of the body was such that the police retained custody until positive identification could be established through fingerprints, which took the incredible time of one month.

"I called the morgue every day. They kept telling me not to come down. They were afraid I'd want to see the body and they didn't think I should because of its condition. I did go there one day to see his belongings myself." (BANKS 2.1.5)

Thirty days later, Mrs. Banks gained custody of the body and received the official death certificate with its unexpected information that her husband's death had been labeled a suicide. It read: "Struck by MBTA train while walking on tracks in a state of acute depression." For the time being, it is sufficient to note that Mrs. Banks initially assumed that death had been accidental, and second that she had doubts about the findings reported one month later on the death certificate.

Initial Reactions

Seven men who had been dying socially were now physically dead. Their penultimate communications were distant, their ultimate ones mainly violent. While they were staging their deaths, their wives had been building new lives. Mrs. Banks, Mrs. Zack, and Mrs. Grenon were actively involved with other men. Mrs. Jefferson was looking around. Mrs. Miller and Mrs. Morneau were not interested in other men. All except Mrs. Codman were in active transit from their married status. They were now pulled back from various distances from their husbands by his final act; all perhaps but two, who were beyond recall.

The reality of social death is most clearly shown by Mrs. Miller, who by all accounts had most put her husband out of her life. She learned of her husband's attempt on a Sunday, and finally went to the hospital six hours later.

"Uh, well then I came home and just waited. I kept calling up. Finally I called——it was about eleven thirty, Tuesday morning, the doctor said he just passed away a few minutes ago, never gained consciousness."

Did you go to the hospital?

"No. They told me not to go down, there was no need to go down, just to send in an undertaker."

What did you do when the doctor told you that on the phone—that he had just passed away?

"Well, I felt kind of bad about it."

Did you cry?

"A little. Uh, yah." (MILLER 9.v.55)

While some would accuse her of being cruel or cold, and others of massive repression, the realities of social death seem far closer to her reality. She had suffered much and watched her children suffer, then finally rid herself of the primary cause of her misery. He had socially died and been buried by Mrs. Miller, and not even his suicide could bridge the chasm between them.

Mrs. Banks also seems not to have been grief stricken in her initial reactions. As we have already seen in considerable detail, she suffered her pain in separating from

George. After his death, she didn't work for three days, but returned when George's body still had not been released for burial. She called the morgue repeatedly. Although she understandably wished to bury her husband without further delay, she did not gain possession of the body for burial until thirty days later. She said she thought—and she had some grounds for believing—that her husband's death was an accident. Thirty days later the medical examiner, to whom neither she nor any other family member had ever given information, ruled her husband's cause of death to be suicide, from "acute depression."

When was the word "suicide" first put to you? When was that idea brought up and by whom?

"It was on the death certificate."

And was that mailed to you, or what? How did you get that?

"Uh, I went down to—did I—wait a minute—how did I get that? No. It was given to me by the funeral director."

Did the word "suicide" come as a shock to you or as a surprise?

"Yah. Like—well, yah, it did. But—I mean, I thought at, you know, I thought it should have been, uhh, 'accident'—myself. But I—"

What was your first reaction when you saw that?

"Oh, I felt terrible."

What did you do?

"I don't know—I think I must have turned white. I
know I felt terrible. I mean I, you know, it was just—it
was like, uh, it was a complete shock to me because I really
didn't expect it. I didn't—I didn't expect that, uhh, that.
And then when I read the CAUSE, you know, 'acute depression,' uh, then I—then I was mad. I got over the shock
and I was mad because, uhh, I mean I, I can't see where,
you know, uhh, anybody can say that—you know. . . .
—And when I saw that, and when I saw 'suicide,' I just
said, oh, you know, like it—it couldn't be. I just
couldn't believe it, because, uhh, I don't think that he was,
you know, the suicidal type. . . . NEVER, never—I never,
no, he never had a death wish, you know, never talked
about it. . . . That's the first thing I, you know, that's the
first thing that hit me when I, when I saw it, and I mean he
had to be, you know, in a pretty, uhh——pretty bad
way to do what he did—if he did that. ——I don't
know, he might have been, you know, dead drunk because
that's all he did was drink." (BANKS 12.VII.61–64)

Mrs. Banks accepted the death but was angry when she
learned that it was considered suicide, or was suicide.
Anger was also the response of another widow.
One of Mrs. Zack's female cousins "had to break the
news to me——poor thing," and afterwards slept with
her because "I didn't want to sleep alone." Before the suicide she had no idea but "then I stopped and thought about
it and I really wasn't [surprised]."

". . . when he died I was so angry and hurt and so bitter about the whole marriage that it's very, very hard for
me to think about him in anything but a very negative . . .
light. . . . I'm sure he probably was trying to say some-

thing like 'See what you did to me. You left me.' Although, who knows? . . . I must admit if we were still living together he probably would still be alive. Yet, for how long? I think suicide was inevitable with Lester because I think he would have failed with whatever he did . . . and I think that ultimately would have led to his suicide. . . . I was hurt about the marriage. Lester was such a lousy husband, you know, for such a long time that it really bothered me, you know, umm. Up until just recently I wouldn't have believed that he loved me, and now I guess, you know, in his own way, I guess, he must have in his own, sick, inadequate way." (ZACK 9.III.47–50)

Mrs. Morneau, who was summoned from the factory where she worked, said she felt:

"First, not—first I was wondering if I done something, uh, some—something I couldn't help him, something I didn't do. If I say something to him to make him mad. I have all kinds of thoughts—always came back. Now I'm all set—I don't have that no more. But the few months, first month—maybe something I should do and didn't do, and to help him, and——" (MORNEAU 13.VII.16)

Age sometimes brings compassion, which Mrs. Morneau demonstrated in this additional reaction.

"Well, you tell yourself then, you know they were sick and [with] something they wouldn't be able to live with. So they suffer, they finish suffering, you know, suffering no more. I, I believe it's the same way with people like my husband that, uh, finally took off his own life; he couldn't bear it no more, you know. He couldn't bear the time and the way he was. . . . But it's hard for the people that's left because it's too fast. You can't accept it; it's hard to accept it. You always think, you always think he gonna come back because you can't believe this. You know, they leave so fast that you can't believe they already left." (Morneau 10.vi.18)

Mrs. Morneau apparently felt some mild guilt, but mainly the relief that her husband "finish suffering." Mrs. Codman said she also felt "relief," adding immediately that it was "a horrible thing to say."

"I think my first reaction was, it finally happened. You know, I could feel something is absolutely inevitable and you can't do anything about it, you're caught in the whirl-pool, you've turned to every possible way——it's finally happened. This is what things were headed for. Uh, I'd drive in the car and say, I wonder if—— How would I feel? It's a horrible way to live." (Codman 15.ix.22)

Her worst fears were now reality and there was a certain relief in that. Mrs. Codman, however, also felt other things.

"You are miserable, you are unhappy, you are lonely, you are angry, you are resentful. Uh, at times you'll cry bitterly and at times you get furious that you did this to me. I mean, not to himself, to me. . . .

"I think you almost get the feeling too, you know, if things were vice versa, he couldn't handle it. That I'm positive of."

Vice versa—what do you mean?

"If something happened to me, I, I can't imagine how he could have handled it——" (Codman 15.ix.27)

To pity, anger, and relief must be added almost pure shock. This was the initial reaction of Mrs. Jefferson, who no doubt was additionally traumatized by discovering her husband. A year later she had this reflection.

"I didn't love him. I suppose if I did, it would have been a major part, but—I don't know—I didn't experience losing someone I loved, I experienced finding a dead body of someone that I knew. Which is two different things— I suppose if I loved him I'd be insane now. I don't know if I could handle it." (JEFFERSON 12.VIII.8)

Mrs. Jefferson had a difficult enough time of handling it as it was.

"I was in a state of shock after that; I was so numb; I was dazed. I just didn't know what I was doing. I started the pills again. I sometimes took sleeping pills before; I couldn't sleep. This was a while ago and I knew I shouldn't start taking them again, but the doctor said I was to have something. So they weren't effective on me. My body was resistant to them and one night I kept taking a bunch of them. I couldn't sleep and I took a whole bottle of them."

Did you know that you were taking a whole bottle and what you were trying to do?

"I wasn't conscious of trying to kill myself. . . . I don't think I was trying to. I can't believe that I was. . . . I lost a whole day, you know. I woke up at Massachusetts General and the whole day was—twenty four hours— it was gone." (JEFFERSON 3.I.2)

The reader should recall that Mrs. Grenon had suffered from severe emotional anxiety at least since high school.

Consequently, her reactions must be interpreted within the context of her unstable life.

". . . when they did tell me, it was almost like unbelievable, like it was happening to somebody else, but really didn't happen to him, you know. It was just like I—like it was happening to some other family, but (laughs) not really happening to—and then when I DID realize that he had done it, it was just a HORRIBLE thing that was—you know, the feeling of it would just start at my toes and it would just work, you know, right up through my body, and I realized that I couldn't stand it, to think about him doing this." (GRENON 12.IX.5)

News of death was shocking, but the manner of death shocked even more. The thought of her husband's suicide was simply not acceptable.

". . . the thought of . . . when, oh, I remember one time I was driving to work and just out of the clear blue sky, this just overWHELMING thing, you know, it just swept over me—what HE HAD DONE, and I, I just thought, OH, I'm going to go MAD." (GRENON 12.IX.5)

"And I remember saying over and over, 'Oh my God, it's all my fault; it's all my fault.' I just kept saying this over and over again, and. . . .
"Oh, guilt, of course——you know the guilt—— really uhh, and that's why I wouldn't let myself think of it, I'm sure, because I felt responsible, and uhh, although, you know, logically the doctor would say to me, 'Martha, you know this is not so. You've been through many years of this; you tried everything; you did nore than you possibly could do, and you did more than you could really stand,' and you know the psychiatrist told me this and the

doctor told me this, and the lawyer told me this, and everybody was telling me, you know, and told me YEARS ago to walk out of the situation and never think about it again. But I still feel, you know, that IF I had been there, POSSIBLY, if I had been there——I might have prevented, or if I'd been caring for him and looking out for him and not just——shutting him off from the family and that sort of thing." (GRENON 12.IX.12–14)

Thus only one of these seven women initially reacted with the guilt feelings that some authorities say suicide characteristically provokes. Two displayed considerable anger, and a third anger mixed with relief. Another also reacted with relief from the pressure she had been living under. Shock immobilized only one, and it was in that state that she attempted suicide. No doubt her discovery of her husband's body, plus the fact that she was only eighteen years old, intensified her reactions. Finally, one woman felt "kind of bad about it."

Ceremonies

The socially impoverished lives of these seven men was clearly evident at the various wakes, funerals, and other services held for them. Some people may have stayed away from feelings about suicide, but primarily, few mourned the loss of these men.

Only the family, a friend of Mrs. Miller's, and her husband's landlord attended his funeral. Five months later Mike Miller had no marker on his grave, no one had visited it, nor had anyone cried over him. Many widows reported difficulty in surviving traditional holidays because everyone was reminded of the missing member, but Mrs. Miller said her holidays were better since he wasn't around to spoil everything. Warming to this theme she continued:

"Yah. Even the day he was buried, my daughter, she had to go to the prom night and she had everything ready and the boy had everything ready so the undertaker said to me, 'Let the child go,' he said, 'because it's such an important night for her and it's not her fault.' So, uhh, I said to her ——I felt so bad for her because she had rushed in town after school to get her hair done and I said, 'Kate, it's too bad this had to happen.' And she said, 'Well, he always had a habit of spoiling things anyways.' " (MILLER 9.v.37)

Added to this bleak remembrance of their alcoholic husband and father were these remarks:

Do you talk about Mike much with the kids? Does he come up?

"Once in a while; they'd rather not talk about him."

How have the kids changed since he's been out of the house? Would you say?

"They seem much happier. They really do. More content. Yeah."

How about yourself?

"Oh I feel much better." (MILLER 9.v.59)

Only the family, and in one case a friend of the widow, were present for the burials of Mr. Banks, Mr. Morneau, and Mr. Jefferson. As with Mr. Miller, the quick and quiet simple ceremonies had less to do with the fact of suicide than with the few people who felt bereaved.

A few of Mr. Zack's fellow students attended a brief memorial service for him with Mrs. Zack and her friends.

His parents later arrived for a short service at the funeral home. Their brief visit was the occasion for an ugly scene; the icy silence was broken only by recriminations blaming Mrs. Zack.

Mrs. Grenon and Mrs. Codman had many friends; they turned out to support the widows through the burial services, along with about a dozen friends of the dead men.

Although a number of friends came to two of the ceremonies for the deceased, in five cases these men passed out of life as they had lived it—alone.

The Search

Mrs. Miller has already indicated that she and her children felt happier after Mr. Miller had finally passed completely out of their lives.

After getting over her initial anger, Mrs. Banks next went through a period of blaming herself.

"I kept——thinking about this, you know, 'for better or for worse,' you know, like should I have—I stuck it out SO LONG, why didn't I stick it out just a LITTLE while longer? You know, things like that were really messing up my mind, you know——"

Did you talk these things out?

"Oh, yah, I blurted them out to Fran (laughs)— anybody that would listen to me, really. —And everybody kept saying, 'Well, now you know, that's not right,' —which people will say, you know, even if they think that you are right, you know, at a time like that . . . this feeling that I get except my, except my girlfriend, who, I told you is very objective and she says, 'Listen—'you know, she got very stern; she said, 'After all—' and she, she kind of, uhhh, she kind of got me out of it—because—she got very angry at me at one point, you know, and she said, 'What are you torturing yourself?' Like, she says, uhh———she said, 'Even now,' she said, 'he's got the best of you, he's gotten the best of you.' She said, 'You know, you've got to—be realistic.' She said, 'Even now, he's gotten his way with you.' And I says, 'How?' And she says, 'By doing what he did.' " (BANKS 12.VII.27)

While Mrs. Banks's friend was apparently sure that George had committed suicide, Mrs. Banks wasn't so sure.

Have you thought more about the manner of his death? I don't know whether you've ever come to the conclusion yourself that it was a suicide or an accident or what.

"No—and I haven't thought about it. There's no way to decide that. I haven't talked to my lawyer about it—I don't know what's happening with it."

If it was a suicide, what would be the reason for it?

"———It could be to spite me. He was a spiteful person, and he knew that would hurt me. And it DOES hurt me—if it was a suicide. And I'M not saying it was—I'll never know. But he was capable of doing it for spite—and yet, there was the note in his wallet—the note said 'I love you,' with nothing more. And yet, could he have loved me and done such a thing?" (BANKS 10.V.42)

How could he have? Why? What did I do? What should I have done? These and other questions went through the minds of six of these seven widows during their search for an acceptable explanation. The fact that they were already distancing themselves from their husbands when they committed suicide made their search for an explanation less intense than that experienced by the other widows, as we shall later hear. Nevertheless, these questions could not be answered; remaining unresolved, they gave rise to anxiety.

"Well, I'll tell ya, I wasn't—no matter where I went or what I did, I just wasn't—if I was here, I, I, if I was in one place, I'd get, uhh, nujjey; if I was at my, uh, girlfriend's I felt well, gee, that gee—but after I was there awhile, uhm, I got restless—anywhere I went, I was very restless."

And was that unusual for you?

"Yah."

And what about reading?

"Oh, I couldn't read. Oh, no."

Because I understand that you like to.

"Yah, I, no, I couldn't do anything, uh, yet, you know, and yet I didn't do that much thinking, but I, uhh—it's uh, it was like a, uh, a caged animal, you know. —I wanted to be at work; when I was at work I was restless; and when I was at Fran's—anywhere that I went, I was very restless; and tense, very restless and tense."

And what about the physical aspects of it? Did you have any special things going on that way?

"Uhh—no, I was exhausted all the time though. (BANKS 12.vii.43)

Repeated thoughts of his death induced thoughts of their own death, but in only one case by suicide.

"There were moments—there were times when things seemed so blue that I felt I could understand how someone felt who took his life. I'm not a suicidal person; I've always been optimistic by nature, active, involved; yet there are times . . ." (CODMAN 3.1.15)

When death takes someone close to us, to think of our own death is not an unusual reaction. In reacting to suicide, perhaps it was not unusual for this woman to think of her own death by suicide. Two other women also thought of their own deaths, but not in terms of suicide. Shortly after her husband's death, Mrs. Morneau made out her will. The other widow who said that her husband's death made her think of her own was Mrs. Zack.

Did it set you thinking about your own death at all?

"Oh, God, yes. That is one of the MAJOR, MAJOR, major, major, major, uhmmm, effects his death had on me, and I probably will never get over that. I'm VERY conscious of the fact that we never know when you're gonna go—even though he didn't die in an accident, and what not, and it was at his own—(deep sigh)—you know, he took his own life, and he made the decision to end his life, and what not, but I am very, very conscious of the fact, you never know when you're gonna die; and, if anything, it's given me a big push to really enjoy my life because who knows when it will be over, you know. And I think I'm more— more—I think about death more now than I ever did. I mean death never meant anything to me. To a certain degree, it still doesn't, because it's hard for me to believe— I don't know if I told you this before—one day I was walking down the street, and I thought I saw him. Here I am, actually saying 'The bastard's still alive' or whatever, and I said, 'Oh, my God,' you know. You know, if I hadn't—viewed the body, I probably never would have believed it, really you know, thinking back, it's like we never lived together; it's like he moved away or something, you know." (ZACK 14.VI.14)

Disbelief is also a common reaction to any death. Five of the seven women reported difficulty in believing their husbands were dead. Like Mrs. Zack, they reported that they thought they had seen him. Mrs. Jefferson said she kept seeing her husband in Europe, where she had gone for a vacation on his insurance money. Since six of the seven husbands had been away from their wives for periods of time even before their separations, they said it was particularly difficult to believe that his current absence was due to his death.

". . . I was thinking a little bit today, thinking back through the year and how I felt compared to how I felt a year ago. ——And—I think, you know, in the beginning when my husband died——of course he had such a long history of illness and being away [in] different mental institutions and drying - out places and——different hospitalizations that he'd had for physical illnesses and one thing or another, he'd really been away quite a bit—— and it wasn't a sudden shock to have him be gone, you see." (GRENON 12.IX.3)

Two of the five disbelievers had viewed the body, three had not. Among the two believers, one had viewed the body. Apparently, seeing or not seeing the body does not make much difference to what the widow believes.

By their own estimates, the shock, the disbelief, and the

relief wore off from a few days to as long as four months later. It was then that the search for an explanation became central. Among the reactions we have reviewed thus far, only this search for an explanation characterized most widows. Yet even here there are wide variations. Mrs. Morneau's search was undertaken almost immediately, conducted empirically, and concluded before most others had even begun.

What did his family say about his dying? Did anyone say anything?

"No. No. No, They know that, they know that he was sick. They were surprised like me because————but me, I was not—too, too surprised. I was surprised in a way, but you see, but he had tried one time and not only that, you know, I find out by myself that thing he done before that I didn't realize, that he had that in his mind for quite awhile."

How did you find that out?

"Well, you see, for some time I know that he was a good man and he thought that he was making trouble for everyone. He thought he had no more friends, he was just making trouble for everybody and he could do nothing about it. And, I know he wants me to have something ————he know that not being by myself————I mean, uhh, he wanted to make sure that something that———— everything that he has——uh——would still belong to me. Because I find how————you see, that house we have up at the lake there, I always thought, myself, I always forget, you know, to put everything————I thought that was only in his name; I didn't think my name was on it. And when I look at all the papers——I have a little chest, you know, where I look at all the papers. He was drinking coffee all the time. And when I look at that paper to find out——to see——the two names was on it, I, the paper was full of coffee so he must have—— when he was alone at home there, he must have took that chest and looked to see if the house, to see if that was on both names." (MORNEAU 4.II.30,31)

Mrs. Morneau shortly thereafter said she "accepted everything," the suicide as well as the death, and indeed so it seemed to us. She had permitted her husband to drink and his alcoholism had drained the family's resources. Yet she had worked and cared well for their children and in other ways minimized the impact of her husband's problems. She had kept her silence with him but took over the family.

Without doubt her rapid and healthful recovery stemmed from her vigorous ancestors and her French Catholic culture. Mrs. Morneau also says she benefitted from the isolating effects of the New England winter. She went back to work at the factory after five weeks, but otherwise had little communication with anyone other than ourselves.

". . . the friends——I didn't see them, you know, for a long time after . . . I didn't talk to them because most of the time I was not here and when I came back here, I was working all the time, and then came winter, and I didn't see anybody. I didn't see nobody for a long time." (MORNEAU 14.VIII.8)

Mrs. Morneau found her answer on the title to what was now her house. Six of these seven widows searched, but each did so in their own ways and with their own list of possible - acceptable explanations.

"I think I have, umm, really kind of deep religious beliefs myself and I was glad that I did have when my husband died because I think I, umm, really had accepted. I must have because I had really accepted within myself the fact that it was life after death. For instance, this was not just something that I wanted to believe in, as a way to make myself feel better; I mean I really seriously believed in life after death and I think that it made the whole process of his dying much more easy for me to accept because I did feel very strongly this way, and uh, I mean to me probably it wasn't such a final thing so that I could accept it within myself a lot more easily." (GRENON 3.II.16)

Even though Mrs. Grenon believed in life after death, she still felt forced to search.

"I'll watch this older couple—I think this gets to me quicker than anything—is to see an older couple walking along the streets, you know, and I say to myself I'll never be there. And I go through all these thoughts of, well, if I hadn't done this, or had done that, and I know this is natural to anybody who has lost—anybody— that you can always look back and see all these things that you wish you didn't do (laughs). But I think perhaps, that in a normal death, of a person who dies of illness that is not caused by anything, except illness, except the body deteriorating, it seems to me that it happens to you, that you can accept the sort of death, and in your involvement in it, but in a suicide type of death, you cannot push aside that part of your mind that says why did I do this, or why didn't I do that, or what was he thinking of, or all the things that lead up to it, or the things that you could think of that happened in the past." (GRENON 4.III.12)

"You know, and I won't be content until I rip every bit of it, every day of that madness apart, and, get it down pat. Then, and only then, will I be able to really come out of it. I don't remember all, I have a bad memory, I don't remember like really little tiny things. . . ."

Do you think those little things would matter?

"Yeah, well everything would matter. Our relationship as a whole, then breaking it down————"

If you had left him—?

"If I had left him first [that is, left him alone], I wouldn't have felt this guilty, I don't think. Um . . ."

Why do you feel guilty?

"Sometimes I think if I had just let him alone, in the first place, nothing would have happened." (JEFFERSON 5.II.28)

The agony of the search went on and on, driven by needs deep within each widow.

"I must go over the way he—he ended his life; I probably go over that, you know, two or three dozen times a week—my mind goes over that and the thought that, like for instance, oh what was he thinking of and, you know, what awful thoughts did he have, you know, just before he killed himself and was I responsible or wasn't I or was it something beyond me or wasn't it." (GRENON 3.II.40)

How do you shut it off? Without some kind of acceptable explanation it is extremely difficult; yet explanations need answers they cannot have.

"I have to admit to the fact that the material [the poison] was there for his use and had been there for weeks, and there was nothing that he would normally have used in the laboratory with the experiments that he was doing at the time. It, it was normal laboratory stuff but nothing that he was working on that would have needed, uh, this particular [cyanide] . . ."

So he specially procured it?

"So he had, I have to face this that he specially had it just— . . ."

Do you know when?

"Some time in February and, uh, now whether he didn't get rid of it because he didn't know if he'd ever really want to use it or whether it was kind of a crutch for him, that if things get too bad I [he] could finally say the hell with it, I, I can't answer. I, uh, well I'll never know the answer which I guess—it's very hard not to know the answer." (CODMAN 6.III.41)

The search led Mrs. Grenon, alone among these seven widows, to seek answers in extraordinary communication.

"You know I do a little of this psychic writing (laughs)—I told you I did."

You touched on it.

"And the funeral of this particular older woman did bother me . . . the husband of this wife is left all by himself, no children—the two of them were really close. And I was feeling really upset for him, so I picked up my pencil . . . so I said well, I'll try some psychic writing. So I was sitting there with the pencil, in my hand—I had paper—and the writing came through to me—'Aren't funerals terrible. In fact the people who are left behind feel so much worse than the people who have gone ahead' is what it came out in the psychic writing. And I laughed, because I was sitting there feeling pretty sniffly to myself, watching this poor little thing (laughs)." (*Interesting*.) "I know, it is interesting, I remember telling the psychiatrist that I did this at one time, 'You don't think I'm losing my mind because I do this, do you, you do't think I'm really going mental or anything like this do you?'" (GRENON 5.IV.27)

"Since my husband died I've had a few writings, and one was to the effect that my husband was not sorry that he had killed himself—as a matter of fact he had more peace than he'd had in a long time. He was sorry that he'd left the family in such a mess. One of the things that came through to me. And another thing that came through to me was—not to dwell on the fact of his killing himself, what he did, which I could not get out of my mind for such a long time. And still can't at times, I still think about it. That he had been so drunk, when he did it that he did not even know what he was doing. Now, probably, if someone was to pull that apart, they'd probably say that was my subconscious mind wishing that's what happened."

How do you feel after this?

"Well, I feel as though there were someone there that I could talk with, and to. And someone I can turn to, you know, and I can think of things that are really close to me that perhaps I wouldn't talk about with anybody else. And I get an answer too. This is very nice. Course I've always been an only child—no brothers and no sisters, and nobody that I can talk to, this is perhaps that it is my subconscious answering in some sort of a way, that, I don't know, comforts me, I don't know."

Don't think you should try to analyze it too deeply.

"I know it (laughs)" (GRENON 5.IV.29)

The *solitary* nature of the search must also be added as nearly universal among these seven widows. They are alone at this time just as they have been much of their lives. They didn't want to go out, feared the questions people would ask for which they knew they had no answers, and felt "like a fifth wheel" among their old married friends. They also realized that their friends did not know what to do or say either. Some friends avoided the subject, while others pretended that nothing had happened. Mrs. Codman said that while she realized "they were trying to be kind," "they were trying to be helpful," it was "neither kind nor helpful." I asked her how she wanted others to react to her and she said, "Just like any other human being." She paused, then added, "I guess that says it all."

Subsequent Reactions

From their initial anger, guilt, relief, and shock they went into isolation and the search for an explanation. For each woman the length of these periods varied from a week or so to three or four months. Excerpts from the interviews allow us to focus on their experiences as they had them, and the sequences in which they came. The length of time any one widow spent in shock or in isolated searching varied with the context of her life, as it did with the context of her husband's death, irrespective of the uniformities of the labels we assign to life and death. All seven husbands died by suicide, but they all died at different distances from their wives.

After their initial reactions, including those experienced when burying their husbands, they searched for a time before the pattern of their lives changed again. For some this change entailed a radical departure from their previous isolation, for others it was characterized by a more subtle change in mood. Mrs. Codman initiated activities.

How long were you numb?

"Oh, I bet it was a good month."

A good month.

"——I found myself absolutely——I couldn't stand the four walls, I couldn't stand to be at home, I couldn't stand to go out, you know, you just uh, and I just, I said, 'Okay, one formula worked for you once; it's going to work again.' Not really believing it (not clear)."

You went from being numb into plunging into things?

"Just trying to——yeah. Plunge. I started to look into schooling, the sisterhood thing came up, which I said yes to, I never would have said yes in a million years (laughs) at any other time, uh, anything that would keep me busy I said yes to (not clear)." (CODMAN 15.IX.28)

"It was the doing first, and the thinking afterwards. It worked for me before. I'm sure that I am running from it, but not to the point that I feel I'm always going to run. I'll be able to look back and pull myself up short, and be fairly sure of where I'm going." (CODMAN 8.IV.9)

"Now Tuesday night——I was out to dinner Tuesday, I went bowling Wednesday, I went out for dinner on Thursday and I never do this. I went to a dance on Friday with a friend and Saturday I had a bridge game, Saturday night at the house."

Oh my, it was a very, very busy week. (laughter)

"And you know, Sunday morning I said, 'Caryl, you're tired and that was the best thing you did.' Because I just, I was out of the funk (laughs) and I really was in one. . . . And I found that having these people in Saturday, there was just the four of us, uh, it was the first time that I had any company, other than family, since my husband died. And it was very pleasant. And it wasn't old friends, married couples, that I, well, I did have, uh, uh, some people in before, you know, former friends—" (*Oh, yes.*) "—or rather friends that I, married friends that my husband and I had been friendly with and it was a most uncomfortable evening, uh, this was a situation where there were four of us, none of us attached to anybody, and we were playing bridge——my daughter had a few friends in too, and it was a very pleasant evening and there was no——feeling of discomfort." (Codman 9.v.32–39)

Mrs. Codman thus rested her mind with forced activities, but the other six women just plain rested. Some took vacations elsewhere—Mrs. Zack went to Bermuda, Mrs. Jefferson went to Europe, and Mrs. Morneau spent five weeks at her son's home. Whether they traveled or not, they wanted some peace and quiet after what they had been through.

"I find now that I can't stand having anybody hovering around me or pressuring me into doing anything. I want to do it in my time and when I'm ready . . . people say to me, 'Well, I know you're lonely,' I'm really not. I'm not the least bit lonely. Because, meanwhile I like the solitude. . . .

"Some people have to have something going. Like the television, even if they're not watching it or the radio or the record player. I can turn all of them off and sit and read or do my housework. And I'm not lonely . . . Janie, she says 'Why don't you come up and spend the weekend, come up Saturday night after work, you must be lonely.' I'm not lonely, I'm really not. I mean I will go and spend a weekend, not because I'm lonely, but because I enjoy her company." (BANKS 10.v.17,18)

"I, uh, just want a vacation."

A vacation from what?

"Emotional entanglement of any kind." (JEFFERSON 12.VIII.18)

Reinvolvement

Although it is now less than two months later for Mrs. Miller but more than six months later for Mrs. Jefferson, they and the other five widows now begin to reinvolve themselves in life. Decisions began to be made by these women who earlier had been incapable of deciding anything including, quite significantly, decisions about their husbands' remaining things.

What about his belongings and his clothing?

"I finally gave everything—one of my brothers-in-law, the one that took care of my lawn all summer—I was talking with her, you know, his wife, one time and she was telling me, 'You know that they, they take up both, they're both the same size.' So, she was talking about it, so I said, 'I'd be glad to give it to John if you think John—' 'Oh,' she said, 'John'd LOVE to have it.' So they came one night and then we went through everything and he took everything—even the shoes, EVERYTHING. So I was glad —it's still like in the family and he can use it, and some that he can't use, I told her—I said, 'If you know somebody that can use it.' She said, 'Don't worry; I take care of it.' I was glad; they came one night and we went through everything. Mmm." (MORNEAU 14.VIII.10)

They were now able to answer the questions people would inevitably ask them as they began to live again.

What do you tell people when they find out you are a widow?

"It depends on the person. Like if I don't know them, I tell them he was sick. My mother told someone he was sick—mentally. So I think sick covers it."

Do you tell people he killed himself?

"Some people. People that are close to me, and people that I like and don't want to lie to."

And how do these people react when you tell them?

"No one understands it. No one could——understand why anyone kills themselves. Understands how I could feel now." (JEFFERSON 12.VIII.8)

"Yeah. Well see, I'm, I'm a funny kind of person. I really don't care what people think. You know, and in a way I sort of get a perverse kick, out of, you know, shocking somebody. You know, you know, I think if they're that uptight or that straight or whatever, you know, well fine, you know, I don't care." (ZACK 9.III.35)

As they reinvolved themselves they experienced themselves in a new way, particularly with respect to other men.

"Friends of mine had me over for dinner Saturday night (laughs)—and they were talking about another friend of mine who recently married and they had her over for dinner too, and so they said to me, um, 'Would you mind if we intro—if we brought some—. Oh, what did they say, they, they had thought about someone they wanted to have for dinner, a single man they wanted to have for dinner to keep me company but they weren't sure of how I would feel about this. (*Uh - hum.*) And I said, 'Well, I don't mind, but don't let it worry you, because I really, you know, I'm not looking for a man, actually.' And so the man said, 'Well, you're sure different than your friend Jackie.' And then they started laughing, because my friend Jackie, I guess, had——and a lot of women, I believe, are like that that are left alone and the first thing they want to do is to find another man. And I honestly don't feel like that. So uh—" (GRENON 8.VI.27)

Once they began to enter the outside world they also learned of our society's other assumptions about widows.

". . . I don't know why it aggravates me, and it shouldn't, but I don't know why men think that if you have been married that if you're not married now that— you have to be hard up for sex." (BANKS 12.VII.57)

Mrs. Codman said she was left alone in a bar one day for a few minutes during which time three men tried to pick her up. This angered her and she bemoaned "the fact that a woman cannot go into any bar in Boston without being considered a pickup by the men there."

She went to the Symphony alone one night, but did not find it pleasant to be alone. She then went on to say that a woman can't even travel by herself, for instance abroad, without feeling "uncomfortable" (CODMAN 8.iv.6).

One solution practiced by some of the women was to form a single new relationship.

"Uh, yes, well Enrique is an old - fashioned, dominating kind of—what he says goes——he's in control of the situation at all times, he relieves me of the burden of deciding what to do, where to go, how to do things—— Lester was so wishy - washy, he never could make up his mind, he couldn't decide so I would have to take it on ——I didn't like it. See, Lester's trouble was that he intellectualized everything——he was good at talking around something——not doing it. Enrique's older." (ZACK 10.iv.2)

"He, um, totally supports me, I know, you know, it's that kind of thing where he just pays the bills and I have no idea of what he is making. You know. Um, he brings the paycheck home, and you know, if there's a bigger bill than usual then it'll go for that or, you know, in that month if we don't have any bills then we'll put it in the bank or we'll spend it or whatever, you know. It's our money, not his or mine . . ."

This is quite a big switch actually, that you are now being supported totally and before you were supporting the two of you.

"Everything. Right."

How do you feel about this?

"I like it (laughs). I mean, if we needed the money, for me to go to work, I would. With Enrique I really feel that, you know, the two of us are doing something together. If I had to go out to work and support him, it wouldn't be the kind of a thing like Lester because Enrique has given me so much and I don't specifically mean money . . ." (ZACK 9.III.31)

Even though four of the seven women did form a sexually intimate relationship with a man for a period, none of them were willing to consider remarriage.

"Well, he knows that I am not ready to form any kind of strong relationship at this point (laughs)."

How does he know that?

"We've discussed it. This we've discussed. And uh, he understands completely." (CODMAN 9.V.55)

"I can't think of anyone I can go to bed with. Manny came over and we went to bed and I couldn't ball him—he couldn't understand." (JEFFERSON 12.VIII.17)

". . . this is the way I feel. This is the way I think now. Um, I think that he did me wrong. I mean, even as far as my relationships, you know, he's just killed it for me, as far as other men are concerned."

In what way?

"Well, I'm very anti - men. To the point that the only way I would want to have a relationship with a man would be if I were feeling something other than, I mean, maternal, you know. I feel like I've been used and I can never really love somebody for themselves and I don't think I'll ever really change." (BANKS 10.v.15)

"No, as far as men are concerned, he has absolutely— hah—sorry, I have a big problem on that; I mean I just, I can't, uhm, I enjoy their company——but——I, I, you know, as far as sex is concerned——I just—I don't think I'm ever going to be able to feel that way about a man again. ——And I hope this is temporary. But I mean I, I've met lots of men, you know, and as long as they're joking with me and I can joke back with them, it's good. But as soon as anyone puts his hand on me, I just —I freeze up."

It just turns you off?

"It turns me off completely."

Have you tried, you know going any distance with some particularly interesting man to see if you could, you know, get yourself warmed up or interested?

"Yes, I have. Yes, I have, but it's not good." (BANKS 12.VII.46)

"I might if I get lonely enough, but I, I really don't think so. I sort of feel jinxed for one thing. And uh, I just don't think it would be important enough to me to take a chance on——walk into another mess (laughs). Because, you know, that was bad enough. And I certainly loved my husband when I married him. But—I don't think I'd care if I never remarried again——I'd rather stay single. . . . I don't think I'm that great a wife that I want to—you know, ruin somebody else's life (laughs)." (GRENON 9.VII.35)

Their reentry was thus not without its problems and some of these would no doubt remain problematic for a long time. Yet their lives were definitely on the upswing.
Reinvolvement frequently included the making of new friends, particularly for the widow who now felt uncomfortable with the old crowd of married friends. Frequently the friends are also widows.

"I have a friend who has been a widow for ten years. I have another friend who has been divorced for four. I have another friend who is recently a widower, almost the same time that my husband died, I think it was the three anyhow, and another friend that I know who has been a widower for two years." (CODMAN 10.VI.4)

On the road to recovery and the reconstruction of a new life, old friends are also often left behind since they remind one of the past. In this transitional period, the widow has a special set of needs, ones generated by her trauma. Progress can therefore sometimes be seen when she begins to leave these temporarily needed relationships. As we have already observed, none of the women wanted an involving heterosexual relationship during their recovery period. If they lacked self - confidence but wanted an outlet, a married man therefore became the predictable choice. He is especially safe if his community position is such that divorce is out of the question. This is what Mrs. Grenon did. She had an affair with the Sunday school superintendent. He had been married for thirty - five years, had five mostly grown children, and dispensed care to the needy of the church.
Nine months later Mrs. Grenon bought a house.

"I just felt that for once in my life I wanted to make my own mind up to something. (*Uh - huh*.) And if there was something that I decided to do, it was important for me to go ahead and do it." (GRENON 8.VI.12)

Do you also feel some sense of a kind of new—?

"EXACTLY. That whole thing to me feels like I'm just starting a, a new way for myself. I really feel moving into this house represents to me——all right——this is the end of this and the beginning of something else . . ." (GRENON 9.VII.6)

". . . Well, it's just that, I think because my husband had died I felt that I wanted to have a completely new kind of life. You know, I wanted to have a new life—— that was somehow disconnected from the other one altogether—because the other one represented to me nothing but misery and agony and unhappiness and sickness and everything that was only, at that time, bad memories to me. And I just had a feeling that if I could suddenly do something completely different that all this would just be a thing of the past and I could start it all over again with a fresh, clean slate." (GRENON 12.IX.24)

So she started a fresh, clean slate, leaving even her married lover behind. You can almost hear her sigh of relief as she now proceeds.

"It's an awful thing to say, this is a terrible thing to say, but I think that all of a sudden a tremendous sense of relief has come over me that this is behind me. . . . And it's not that, you know, I'm not happy that he's gone or that you know, I'm glad for his death, as far as he himself is concerned, I mean, if he had been well and happy, still living,

then great. But it's a relief of the responsibility, I think."
(GRENON 9.VII.16)

While reintegration brought other problems, it also brought release from the old ones. The extent of the widows' release will be evident in their reactions a year from the day of the suicide.

A Year from THAT Day

All members of the research staff had now been engaged in interviewing our research volunteers for nearly a year. Throughout the series thus far we had primarily listened to whatever the widow wanted to talk about, asking questions about the material they introduced. In what we called the *Annual Interview* we shifted our approach somewhat. Just after a year from *that* day, we asked them to review their year with us, probing for their perceptions of themselves and the changes through which they thought they had gone. Not every woman was able to do so, and as always we followed their lead. Continuing to let them tell us how it was, let us listen to their retrospectives, tracing with them their path to survival and locating their current position.

Well, Mrs. Miller, in looking back over the year, how do you think you've changed since the time he died, until now?

"Changed?"

In your feelings——well, one of the things you said was you're thinking less about him.

"Yes."

Another is, what kinds of things you're thinking?

"Nothing particular, really, you know? ———"

Still a mixture of some bad things, some good?

"Yes."

More one than the other?

"As the time goes by, you seem to forget, you know?" (MILLER 12.VII.14)

So, what do you plan for an anniversary mass: Can you explain what that entails?

"Well, we're planning to go to the church for the mass and then we're planning to visit the grave, because nobody has been to the grave yet, and then I'm planning to have them back to the house afterwards." (MILLER 11.VI.13)

Who would be coming back to the house besides the Millers? No one we ever found out anything about. Mr. Miller died without a single friend, including his wife and children, and all were better off without him.

Starting out the year with more distance from her husband than anyone else, a husband who had died socially from her life already, he was of such little importance to her life that she did not mourn at all. Had we been interviewing her while she was separating from her husband she might have had more to tell us. As it was, our questions about her reactions largely went unanswered because she had so little to tell us. Yet that same distance that had initially helped her ultimately hindered her full recovery.

One day, an interviewer called Mrs. Miller's house at five P.M. She answered the phone, and said:

"Oh, I'm sorry, I forgot all about calling you. I'm so sorry dear. I haven't been well. Last Saturday, I went out with Kate to visit a friend. I felt fine, we were having some coffee, then I began to feel queer, like I was going to pass out. I asked Kate to take me to the bathroom and I threw up. I felt relieved, we sat down again, and then I passed out. I passed out three or four times. [The police were called.] The policemen thought I was having a heart attack. I was plenty scared, I tell you—especially when I came to and heard the siren and saw Kate crying.

"The doctor at the hospital said that I had very high blood pressure. He said, 'You're keeping something in that's bothering you. I can tell that you're under an awful lot of tension. There's something you're not letting out.' Can you imagine that—and he never even saw me before." (MILLER 11.VI.3)

Mrs. Banks was probably the most abused and long - suffering of all. Undoubtedly she stayed with her George for unhealthy needs within herself. Their life before his death underscores the crushing costs we all continue to pay for the disease of alcoholism, as well as our society's continuing refusal to respond adequately with rehabilitation. He had no life left in him when he was hit by the train, whether his death was suicide or not. And he greatly impoverished the lives of his wife and two step - children before he departed. His illness and what must have been her need for punishment combined to form a bond that only his death could finally break.

"I didn't feel that way while we were living it, it wasn't until after he died, that I was able to realize that it was wrong. Only because I left. I mean even today, I can say well maybe I did do him wrong by not having him put in a hospital. Or even committed because he was doing things that were really weird, you know. Maybe I did do him wrong in that respect, now maybe I did. I mean this is something that I'll never know. Maybe I should have really done something instead of just leaving him, you know.

"But the point is this, that once you're in it, you have to treat this person almost like an invalid. And you can't do that. And love and understanding, they've got to have their own life, and when they slough off you've got to be understanding. You can't do this. I think an alcoholic has to be hospitalized because your family really can't do anything for you. You know, anybody who is that close." (BANKS 10.v.38)

She may be right. Compulsory hospitalization for alcoholics, as required for some who have active tuberculosis, may be the only answer. Clearly, however, silence is not. Her care, rendered through silent coexistence, only allowed the cancer to grow. After sleeping "all the time" for several months while also feeling guilty, she finally began to realize what her husband had done to her.

"It was over pretty quickly because I think, if there's a man around a woman always feels like she's protected— but—when I look back now, I was the one, the protective one, it wasn't he, really.

"Not all of a sudden, but, you know, in the last ten months I began to realize that I am a pretty, well I've always been stable, but he brought me down. Well number one, I was starting to lose my self - respect, for myself as a woman. Other people were losing it for me as a woman."

Why is that? Do you think when they see a man like that they judge you according to him, they don't separate the two of you?

"That's right. I mean in this respect, 'Any woman that lives with a man like that has got to be either stupid or,' they couldn't. Well now I know, I mean I know more now than, I used to think that this is what they used to think. But I know they used to think, 'What's the story, why is that woman doing it?' You know, 'Why's she doing it,' you know, 'What's the story behind it?' Things like that. There's no story behind it really, mainly, I was just stupid and I was just too stupid, and I mean, I did use the word compassionate but I don't know now if I was. All that com—I guess I was. I really felt sorry for him. I mean, I used to hate him with the passion at times, you know, I used to look at him, six feet two, big guy, on the couch there, and I used to feel sorry for him, instead of feeling sorry for myself." (BANKS 10.v.35)

Once she had gotten to this point she could then later reflect on her contribution to his illness.

"The one thing though, that I still do feel guilty about, and I, and I shouldn't, is that I didn't leave him like ten years ago and I would have been a heck of a lot better off and he may have been too. You see? 'Cuz, I couldn't handle him——"

What do you think would have happened to him if you had separated about ten years ago?

"Well, I really don't know, but uh, he was a lot younger then, he had more—self-confidence, uhm, he might have straightened himself out. You know? I don't think he'd ever find another woman though. But basically, I don't think he cared that much about——he thought ——he needed a woman. You know? But I don't think he really cared that, that much about women. A man that drinks doesn't really. That drinks heavily. ——They're very necessary, uh, they're necessary at times, but I don't think that he really, uh——he didn't care that much about women. I'm not saying that they're, you know, they, they turn on to men or anything, but just——they don't have time. They're too, alcoholics are very self - centered, you know? ——" (BANKS 14.VIII.14)

At the end of twenty years of marriage she found herself without family, without friends, without even rudimentary financial resources. But at least she was alone.

"I LOVE living alone. No. I love living alone. Uh—— as far as my attitude towards my husband——yes, it's changed. Uh—I think, uh—he, he did me a terrible injustice all, almost all the years we were married and then he had to do something like this——I don't know, you know, if he did it, the only reason that I——if he did it ——the only reason I think he did do it was to punish me somewhat. They say that most people who commit suicide, I mean that's their, you know, their motive, really. To cast punishment on somebody. Of course, I don't know that he did. ——'Cuz I feel that he, he wrecked he RUINED my life for me." (BANKS 15.IX.34–36)

Mrs. Banks said, "his death defintely made, you know, some kind of mark on me." Notice how the pattern of her life continues through his death. For at least the twenty - first year, the length of her married life, she ignored that her husband's life ALSO had an impact on her. To accept death you also must accept life, and Mrs. Banks has yet to do so. She still wants people to feel sorry for her.

As the wise Mrs. Sullivan put it, "you can only feel sorry for so long." Life does not depend upon sorrow for its living; sorrow also has its limits. Surviving a suicide threatens life itself. In death as in life conjugals mold each other.

Mrs. Miller avoided her experience and so continued to suffer for something she had not done. But she had lived with "that drunk," had been strongly influenced by that twenty - year experience. Her priest did her no favor in getting her to take her husband back when she got rid of him some five years earlier, but it was her decision—a decision that led to other experiences that had their impact. Not accepting her life with Mike Miller, she followed the same trajectory after his death.

What path could we say Mrs. Banks took to survive? She tortured herself, escaped through sleep, suffered through the callous treatment of our public servants, and also learned some basic things about herself and her relationship to her husband. Perhaps we should simply forego any label and just wish her well.

It was not unusual for the widows we contacted to tell us that their situation wasn't the "usual" one—whatever that is. Nevertheless we were able to persuade some of them to participate in our research even though they were "different." Mrs. Zack was particularly emphatic on this point; yet she behaved not unlike many of the others. She cared for her Lester, eventually taking him over. She withdrew her care, was numb after his suicide, and blocked and repressed any positive feelings she had for him. She was angry, bitter, and reluctant to remarry even though she was now living with a man with whom she was quite close.

You mentioned to me earlier that you had kind of soured about getting married again—

"Uh-hum. He [Enrique] talked about marriage. He's, he's um, separated. He has a child. (*I see.*) And um, he's in no position to get married at this, at this time. But he has talked about it. And I don't know. Now, it's hard to think of marriage, it really scares me because at one point I loved Lester. I guess, you know. And yet something happened and we grew apart. And while I can say that I really love Enrique now, I don't know what's going to happen in five years. And people do constantly change, develop and grow, hopefully, and you can't always grow in the same direction."

Well, what about kids? What are your feelings about kids?

"I never want kids."

You never want them? Why not?

"———I'm too selfish. Kids are, um, they just interfere with what you're doing too much. . . . I just, you know, have no desire to have children. I mean, my mother is constantly saying, 'Oh, dear, you'll change.' But you know, I can't really see how I will. I also don't understand this concept of appre—joy that you get from a child. I don't see how a child can bring you joy. You know? Because nine times out of ten when they grow up they become exactly what you didn't want them to do." (ZACK 9.III.32,37)

Lester obviously did not behave according to her plans either. In this, he, or course, was no different from most if not all of the twelve husbands. Suicide does challenge the expectations of everyone associated with the suicide. Since our own self-conceptions are formed in part from others behaving as we think they will, life and death errors in our expectatons of others have nearly equally reactive consequences for ourselves. This may help explain Mrs. Zack's continuing hatred of her dead husband.

You mentioned there were a couple of things that you wanted to tell me about, were there any other things?

"Oh, so the death was definitely one, and the second, oh, thinking of death and the study, and then, uhh, just, uhh, even the fact that whenever I think of Lester, I never have any good thoughts. But this was true when I loved him too, and, you know, I think it's probably a shame. In a way, I mean, you know, there must have been some happy moments together, and my only memories of him were —are bad. I mean, when I think about him, I either have a reaction 'that God damn son of a bitch' or, you know, 'the poor sick devil' you know. But I don't have any kind of a —I can't remember any of the, uh, really good times, the fun—there's no more feeling that I have towards him, and most of the time when I think about him, especially if I don't think of him as dead, it's real hostile feelings. That, that has changed a little bit. I mean, time has a way of healing and I'm happy with Enrique so, you know, all that is over and done with, you know. But, uhh, I don't have any fond memories of him at all, uhh, you know." (ZACK 14.vi.22)

These were nearly her final words to us fourteen months later. Had she accepted his death? His suicide? Would it have been easier had she not been on the way to the divorce court? Perhaps as with Mrs. Miller, her distance from her husband eventually proved negative to her full recovery.

All three of these women had placed some distance between themselves and their husbands at the time of suicide, and so had a fourth, Mrs. Grenon. Recall that she had purchased a house nine months after her husband's death, and things appeared to be moving forward for this deeply troubled woman—until the twelfth month.

Was the anniversary of the death a week or so ago? How was that?

"Well, you know, I wish I could say to you (laughs) that it was a, a terrible day of memories and looking back and all, because as though that would be a more normal way for me to react. In fact, I thought of it since. It seems as though that's what most women would have done. But the day came and went, and I never remembered that it was the day of his death at all . . . until two days later, and I think the reason, part of it was not the reason I ——I was busy; I was working and I was terribly busy that day, and I was—I had no time to think of ANYTHING except what I was doing at my desk and the tremendous pace I was, I was putting in that day. And I was so exhausted when I came home, I DROPPED into bed and fell asleep, and it wasn't until the day afterwards that I thought, my HEAVENS, the twelfth was the day that John died and I NEVER thought of that.

"But, the Sunday BEFORE that was the WORSE for me because my daughter had wanted to have flowers in memory of her father on the altar which we do in our church in memory of people that have died, and, we couldn't have them on the exact date of his death and so we had them on the Sunday before. And we went to church, she and I, and we sat in the back, and THAT is when all of the tremendous memories kept, you know, REALLY flooding into my consciousness of looking back and thinking about the past years, the fact he was gone, and I got more nervous and more nervous, and I get nervous in church anyway because I have a certain amount of—hah—claustrophobia anyway, and I just was—ohh, I was just—I was so nervous that I felt as though I was ready to just jump out of my skin.

"We had a combined service with the Episocopal church that day and the new ecumenical program that we have been combining with other churches. We had a new type of communion service where we took communion up at the rail, which our church does not do; it's usually passed out in the plate by the ushers. So the church was called to come forward and take communion up at the rail, and I was so nervous that—I watched the pews emptying out, and Sarah turned and looked at me and I must have—my face must have REALLY been a sight, because she said, 'Mother, you're going up to take communion, aren't you?' And I said, 'Oh, don't ask me to do that. I can't do that. I can't—I can't walk or do anything; I'm just so nervous.' And she says, 'Why, mother, you can't do that.' She said, 'Peter is up there'—that's the young minister, 'and he's administering communion, and Dad's flowers are on the altar and you just CAN'T sit here.' So, I said, 'Well, all right' because I could see how much it meant to her, and I just felt though it was going to be physically impossible to walk up that aisle; I was just so strung up. But —hah—but anyway, I WENT, and I was so nervous. But the funny part of it was, and the sacrilegious of it was, in our church we don't have wine. We, we drink—it's just grape juice, and (laughs) and they had a chalice, the Episcopal chalice that they were passing and everyone drinks out of this chalice; and I was so nervous but I SWEAR I felt like picking up that chalice and just TOSSING (laughs) the whole thing down (laughs). I just felt like draining it right—I was shaking like a leaf. It was all I could do to get my hands on the, the chalice, and, so I, I stood there. I don't know how I ever stood there but I did, took communion, and went back to my seat.

"But, you know (sighs), something HAPPENED to me; I couldn't think. I, I got out of the church and people were coming up to me and——commenting on the flowers and saying good morning and one thing or another, and a couple of people who I haven't seen all summer said to me, 'Where's your new house, Martha? Where do you live now?' And my mind went COMPLETELY blank, and Sarah said I BABBLED some kind of foolish—(laughs). She said, she said that I didn't even make any sense. She had to step in and say (laughs) 'We live over—' you know, and she said, 'Mother, what happened to you?' She said, 'You REALLY were—were completely not yourself.'

"I don't know what happened to me except my nerves were just shot, and uh, so I think that I relive that day so much and everything was such a disaster to me during that service that I think when the actual day came, you know, uhh, it was just another day for me. And I was glad it was because if I'd started thinking about it in the morning and thought about it all day long, that would have been awful."

How long did it take before you started feeling yourself again?

"Well, it was terrible. I came home and I was so uhh, confused, mentally confused; I really couldn't make sense, you know. My, my mind—and then my son came after church, and he asked me a couple of things and——and I made some sort of foolish answers to him because he said, 'Mother, you're not making any sense. What's the matter with you?' (laughs) You know, and it wasn't until later on in the afternoon that I actually—I think it passed, passed over."

Just gradually?

"Yah, it was just a COMPLETE nervous reaction. It was just like my body wasn't——and my mind weren't clicking at all. That was a bad day (sighs)." (GRENON 12.IX.30–33)

Setbacks do occur.

As noted earlier, not all of our twelve widows could or would engage in a retrospective. The very young Mrs. Jefferson was one of them. She didn't recall details very well, experienced some difficulty in following a single line of thought, and her principal interviewer preferred her own seasoned approach. Nevertheless, the central thrust of the case clearly emerges. First, recall that in part Mrs. Jefferson married her polio - crippled husband for fear her parents, because of her cohabitation, would put her back in a juvenile home. While she did have alternatives, she was inexperienced enough to think she could totally disregard pieces of paper like marriage certificates. Of course the marriage was a mistake from the start and one wishes her parents had been kind enough to just let them live together. A year later she did say:

"Well, at his death I didn't feel anything. Nothing at all—it was familiar in a lot of ways—this feeling of not feeling, then coming out of it. And so I, I don't know what I did, but I——no, it was after, when I was coming out of shock. Like coming out of it felt familiar, when you begin to feel again?"

How long before you felt like that again, coming out?

"Um, the beginning? ——After Europe. That's why I really wasn't in Europe. I wasn't in Europe." (JEFFERSON 12.VIII.6)

When she returned home after having spent, given away, and "loaned" all the insurance money, she hitch-hiked her way to Florida.

"Well, my folks went down there, so I went and crashed in on them. At St. Pete's."

Did you meet anyone there?

"No, I just stayed on, I recuperated. That was my recuperation period after Europe." (JEFFERSON 5.II.10)

In spite of all the people she'd been with, or perhaps because of their numbers, she felt that they all let her down because they wouldn't really talk to her. She said that one girl in particular had been a very close and helpful friend for many years.

"Except when Phil died she copped out (laughs). Uh, she was scared."

How did she cop out?

"Uhmm, she wouldn't talk to me. It was like, uhh, she was afraid she said—I guess she regretted——she couldn't help me in any way. She didn't know what to do and, umm, it's very strange because I needed that so much, at least I thought I did, we, sure I did (laughs). Uh, and yet, you know, you feel as though you need it and yet you're not—there's not anything anyone can do or say that can make you feel better because they don't know what the hell they're talking about." (JEFFERSON 6.III.8)

Mrs. Jefferson said that no one realizes that her getting married caused Phil's death, and that she is very wary about going into marriage a second time. (JEFFERSON 9.VII.5).

Clearly Mrs. Jefferson was able to see some difficult things about herself and her relations to others. I sometimes referred to her as the Intensive Analyzer because she searched for an explanation so long and so intently. Mrs. Jefferson searched and searched, then, largely without any help from others (like the other widows). She stated, believed, and insisted that "I killed Phil."

"Yes, I really felt guilty, I really believed that I killed Phil. Here in this book [diary] I state (laughs nervously) that Phil must die, it must be done. A few months before he died, and from then on, things just started collecting, and uh, I suppose I did—drive him a bit nutty, uh, just through being myself and he couldn't accept it. But I thought I was, uh, like purposely trying to drive him insane, you know, and I wasn't—what I was doing was just showing him more of myself, and each new thing I showed him, it would just mess him up more—and that drove him insane, too, his not being able to accept my showing, and that's why I guess I couldn't accept Phil dying." (JEFFERSON 5.II.18)

Her basic fear, first expressed in the second interview and continuing right through the ninth and last, was that Phil would "drive me insane."

Tell me how you're feeling, inside, since we last talked.

"I don't even remember what we spoke about, last time (laughs)."

I think you were feeling a little lonely, last time.

"Well, everyone's lonely, you know. It's just that I think I realize it more than a lot of people. And when I do that, I think of it too much, and when I think on it too much I fantasize, and I exaggerate, and I make it more and more. And last night I caught myself doing this, and I guess I came out of that, because I caught myself doing it. I'm, I'm scared to sleep alone upstairs."

Here in this house?

"Just this house. I really believe that Phil is haunting me (laughs)."

Tell me about that.

"Um, well I don't know what happens after death, and I can't really say that I do believe in ghosts, or I don't, 'cause I just don't know, but I know that if it is possible, he would come back. And I was talking to Spider about it, Spider sort of believes in witchcraft, and stuff, and he told me to sleep with garlic in the room. And, like, I came home and I just couldn't bring myself to open up garlic and sleep with it in the room. . . . Because I felt absurd, and I said to myself: 'It's mind over matter' because I know he can't hurt me physically and the only thing he could do is drive me insane. And like, one night I was sitting here saying to myself, 'Okay, you can do it, you can do it! I give.' "

How did Phil manifest himself?

"Noises—like I know every noise in this house, and I —it's just a feeling, you know—I really doubt if he's there at all—it's just my head going crazy—(laughs) —only I don't believe I'm crazy."

Do you think of him much?

"I always think of him." (JEFFERSON 5.II.16–18)

No doubt the image of Phil hanging became branded on her memory. It kept reappearing, haunting her.

How do you feel now about the state of your mental health? Are you worried?

"Not really worried—it's just that I don't like the thought of recognizing myself with Phil. I always thought we were two different characters, and we're not."

In what ways are you?

"Uh, I guess in attitude towards people in general. They are different, but they are attitudes. —I don't want to identify with Phil, I don't think I'm trying. It's just sometimes I see something. I dreamt of him for the first time for a long time, the other night. He came back and was alive, and I was a housemother for like a hotel, a whole bunch of kids, and they each had their own room, and I was checking each room to see if they were okay——and in one room Phil was there, and I was quite calm, I said I would be right back, he didn't say anything, and I went to finish the rooms and there was one little girl, a real brat— kicking and screaming and biting—you know the sort d—."

Remind you of anyone you know?

"Oh no."

Maybe of yourself as a kid?

"Oh no, I was a quiet, good little child. I put her in her room and then I went back and out of a window there was silhouette of him hanging——and I said, 'No. No.' And I started yelling for help, but no one came, so I yelled louder 'Help'—and woke everyone up in the house." (JEFFERSON 14.IX.4)

What brings crying on?

"I'm going into the same thing now as Phil—I don't want to be with people, I'm lonely. Phil hated to be alone —I want to be alone, but——I want to live alone, and, and when I say that I mean I think about when he used to live alone and stuff. And the reason he killed himself is that he didn't want to go back living alone, he said he couldn't do it. And that scares me . . ." (JEFFERSON 14.IX.2)

Obviously Mrs. Jefferson has had problems since at least early adolescence. Equally obviously those problems were exacerbated by her unfortunate marriage. Understanding this, no label is needed for her path to survival. Yet that does not prevent us from wishing that her location on the path were higher.

Paths to survival, as we have already observed, vary considerably. Each widow had her own individual life, her own special relationship to her husband, her own unique reaction to his deviant death. Commonality only emerges in the form we identify that undergirds their lives, for example in the care that was needed and that which was given within a relationship.

Mrs. Codman's special burden lay in having been rejected twice, first by her first husband's divorce, then by her second husband's suicide. She "lived on tranquilizers" for eight or nine months and contemplated suicide herself, but to her own surprise managed to survive. A year later she speculated that perhaps he "did it" to provide for her and her children financially, to do at least that much for her. Or it might have been because he didn't feel "an inner worth. . . . He didn't feel valuable in himself." Then she concluded that she would never know why, and anyway "I'm no judge; I don't judge him at all because I can understand."

Mrs. Codman, what did you do April 30?

"———April 30 I went out to dinner with Abe [male friend]. —He called me a couple of weeks before—— he knew the date and——he said, 'We're going out for dinner Saturday night.' I said, 'That's just fine.' ——And we did. We went out to dinner that night. And two days before, on a Thursday, an acquaintance of mine called, who had been helpful when my husband was——oh, he put up shelves for us and she said, 'My husband died.' The funeral was that day, Saturday, which was April 30. And uh, I went to the funeral. I felt I had to go. She bothered to call and tell me about it, because I never would have read it in the papers——I just DON'T read them—— that's what I did April 30."

What did you think about it?

"The funeral was difficult. Uh, of course, it was totally different. These people are Episcopal, and uh, but nevertheless it was a funeral and I didn't like it, uh——it was difficult. I guess I JUST GOT THROUGH the day. And it was very——it helped that we went out that night. We just went for dinner. It's just——knowing I was doing something with someone who totally understood EXACTLY how I felt, wouldn't of cared if I had a good time or I didn't have a good time. I didn't have to make conversation, I could be miserable if I wanted, he didn't care. —And he wasn't, uh, sympathetic, you know, we were just together for that time. It was a very understanding thing to do and it was the right person to be with, better than family, better than anyone else I could imagine." (CODMAN 15.ix.33)

A year from THAT day, Mrs. Codman thus went to a friend's funeral and afterward to dinner with the new man in her life. Like the other women, she was reluctant to get involved again, but nevertheless was well on her way to her third marriage when we last saw her. Life's circumstances, for Mrs. Codman, always seemed to precede her decisions about them, in this instance as in the others.

The indefatigable Mrs. Morneau had her tense moments, her guilty feelings, her sorrow and grief.

I wondered then if you could tell me how you think you are now compared to how you were a year ago?

"Oh, my goodness——it's like night and day. No, now I have peace in myself, you know, now I realize that I done what I could do for him——there's nothing you can do and he couldn't help himself and, uh——it's better that way. It's hard, it's hard, a lot of times I said, I had a lot of hard times with him, you know, then all the time I get mad at him, but still I miss him. I wish he was here just the same, you know, because even if sometimes you said, 'Oh, my goodness.' ——You get so, uh, sick of them, you know, you said to yourself, 'Maybe it be better if he was not here.' But you, you said something like that and you don't realize that uh, you know, that you don't mean it. You don't really mean it——"

So that—

"But now, now, I think of him, now I think of him when he was happy, you know, and hope that he's happy again. I don't think of him like when he was drinking or something like that. I, I don't think of that no more—— not at all."

And do you think your life is better now?

"A little bit. I can, I'm not uh, tense all the time. You see before I was always all tense that he's gonna get hurt, he's gonna do this, he's gonna do that. We, we go someplace sometime, I get scared in the car and uh, no, I don't have that. See, I don't have that fear that I use to have all the time. So that, uh, this, this way, I'm better in a way. But, but uh, not the other way. I wish even if he was sick, I wish, I STILL wish I was with him because it's uh, you're not alone. Even if some people you know that, uh, uh, even if sometime they do something that you don't like, you're still not alone. You still have somebody with you. Somebody that you love with you. Uh, that's, that's what I'm missing." (MORNEAU 13.VII.36,37)

Did you find yourself thinking more, or the same, about him? You know, was it a special day in your mind?

"No, that's just the, uh, the only day, uhh, the one ——I dream of him one night, and it was just, uhh, like uh——I was supposed to go someplace and you know,

when you want to get ready—in a dream when you
wanna get ready, but he was like——when he was living, you know, he never refused me. If I wanted to go
someplace, he was ready—'Okay, I bring you wherever
you wanna go,' and, but you know, in a dream you always
get up before——you can't get dressed or there's something missing and you wake up before——before you
get where you wanna go. That's the only time I dream of
him. And I was hoping, you know, I was always hoping to
dream of him. And I was hoping, you know, I was always
hoping to dream and see him——so many nights."

*And how did you feel after the dream when you woke
up?*

"Oh, I was so glad——I was so pleased that I see
him! . . . EVERY night, every night—before I go to bed,
every night I always pray for him and I——every
night." (MORNEAU 13.VII.5)

Alone among the widows, Mrs. Morneau continued to
give her care to her husband after his suicide. Fourteen
months later she had "two piles that high, it's all [prayer]
books [said for him]. . . . A lot of them are for perpetual
life and then some, a lot of them for twenty - five years,
five years, ten years. . . . I know he have a lot of prayers
but that's something we never have too much." (MORNEAU
14.VIII.21)

Nor does her care stop with prayer.

What about getting busy in organizations?

"Yes, you see, that's one thing I LOVE——I can't now
with no car, you can't go no place. That's why I'm working hard——I'm gonna try and get my license."

Then you can get busy and make friends.

"Then, then, then I like to be busy in AA, to help an AA member and to help the woman that their husband are alcoholic or on pills—to WORK with them. That, that's my dream——if I can realize, you see if I can——you know, if I get my license I can do that—that's, that's— I'm gonna be in heaven. That's what I like to do."

And that way you get to meet people, too.

"Yes, yes, and help them in the same time. Because they ——understand, I can understand them because we were in the same boat, you know. We went through the same thing and I can help them——is something that I know —that I didn't understand at the time, now I can see through now, more through, and I can help them." (MOR-NEAU 14.VIII.37–38)

These plans were on their way to realization the last time we saw Mrs. Morneau. After three unsuccessful tries, she had passed the written part of her driver's examination and was then taking lessons. Mrs. Morneau accepted both her husband's death and his suicide, knew he was planning it both before and after the event, was grieved yet glad that his suffering was over. And she accomplished this by herself as she had always done. But that also has its negative side.

I just wanted to ask you, what would you say would be your major problems, your most important problem right now, or any particular worries that are on your mind?

"Really——before I didn't mind staying alone, and now I, I don't like it—really. Yah, it's funny, huh? After being alone so long, and I wish I had somebody, like, uhh, somebody should stay so I wouldn't be alone. And before, I would NEVER mind; I was alone almost all my life. And now I HATE to be alone, and I didn't want to tell because I don't want—I don't want to go live with my children but I really——if I knew somebody, you know, that want—uh, want to have a home and be with somebody —just to have somebody to talk and discuss and—just to say that you're not alone."

When did you realize that?

"Ooh, a few weeks ago, maybe a month, a month and a half. Yah, I don't like it. Even at night, I wish——"

So, would you take somebody to live, not necessarily family—you mean just some——

"Anybody, you know, that, uhh, uh, you know that wants to, like, a companion, you know, a man or a woman, anybody, as long as—as my age or older or younger, as long as they, they just want—like, you know to be together and—but not to get married again. No. No, that's, that's, uhh, I don't want that—NO, but just somebody that to see I'm not alone." (MORNEAU 14.VIII.36–37)

Summary

Seven men who were dying from the lives of their legal spouses later committed suicide. Some were already "dead" for their wives. The widows' reactions consequently varied according to their previous distance from their husbands. Reactions ranged from pity and relief, to anger and guilt.

Although none had yet been legally divorced at the time of the suicide, that proceeding would have been pure formality for two women, who were already divorced in the important dimensions—the psychological, emotional, and social dimensions. These two widows quite naturally deeply resented being brought back into their former husbands' lives as their widows. They were not bereaved.

The other five had less distance from their husbands, but it was still sufficient for them to blame him. Only one of the seven initially cried, "It's all my fault," and although several others experienced guilt later, that reaction was never universal nor of long duration. In life as in death, their reactions were their own.

The single pattern that emerged, and it had one exception, was the search for an explanation. The widows withdrew into themselves for a period, searched in solitude for an answer they could accept, rested, and then reinvolved themselves in the new lives they had already begun to build. Reinvolvement came within weeks for some and within months for others, and we constructed no time schedule that they all had to fit.

Re-emerging, they all found themselves unwilling to marry again. While some were perhaps past that age, even the eighteen- and twenty-five-year-old women doubted that they ever would again. Even with these strongly felt reservations, two had new men in their lives as we left them, and three others were dating. Life does go on.

THE PHYSICALLY DYING

Social death before suicide was already well underway in the seven conjugal pairs we have just discussed. In the two cases we consider now, physical death was on its way, albeit from natural causes. Recall that Mr. Burke had premature advanced arteriosclerosis of the cranial artery and had been severely incapacitated for more than a year. The transformation of her formerly active husband into a dependent child was so marked that Mrs. Burke could say, "My husband passed away, for me, a year ago" (2.1.3), when he had to retire. Socially he had died out of much of Mrs. Burke's life, and just how much longer he would be around physically she didn't care to know. She was doing what she could to go on living, including doing many things without him.

Mrs. Sullivan also expected her husband to die, but not by suicide. Doc Sullivan "was fine, five or six years. And the last couple of years he got depressed. He wouldn't go out" (SULLIVAN 7.v.7). For her own reasons Mrs. Sullivan did not force him to go out as she had earlier. He spent his time going through his things, then through old letters "that he wrote me in the service," throwing them all away. Perhaps our minds refuse to see what we are unwilling to accept. Not seeing we can then go on. A week before Doc Sullivan's death, one of Mrs. Sullivan's sisters said to her: "He's going to die soon. I see the look of death in his face."

These two widows alone among our twelve thus expected death soon. Anticipating this they had begun to prepare for life without their conjugants. They did not change their relationships to their husbands, especially in the sense of pushing them out of their lives, but instead seem to have marked time while waiting for the death they could see coming.

Unlike the preceding seven widows who were on the way to a separate status from which they were called back, these two women were on their way to widowhood, but from natural causes—they thought.

Their Penultimate Communication

Mrs. Sullivan went to bed after the last television program was over, leaving her husband, as usual, reading in the bathroom.

The Burkes spent the early and mid - morning hours together, then she went with the children to look at a cottage to rent for the summer.

THAT Day

"I blamed myself because I didn't hear him, 'cause I ALWAYS heard him, every night.

"But, uhh, he must have been very sneaky, very soft because I didn't wake up. Because all he had to do was click those crutches and I was awake. I didn't hear a sound. I don't under——he must have sneaked in his stockings or something. I don't know, I just didn't hear him, and that's the only time. Because I can—even now, sometimes I wake right up from a sound sleep because I think I hear the crutches. I'll sit up in the middle of the bed and I'll wonder what I'm sittin' up there for, and I thought I heard the crutches."

Well, he must have gone very quietly.

"He must have been very quiet because he knew—— he'd say, 'I'm only——I'm only going for a ride, go back to sleep.' Because all he—all I had to do was hear that click and I was awake. So he, he knew this, so he must have did it very quietly that I—that he knew he wouldn't wake me." (SULLIVAN 12.x.18)

How did you find out that your husband had died?

"The police came to the door. I went to bed. I got up a couple of times to see if he was all right, he was in the bathroom. The next thing——he always was in the bathroom readin' because he couldn't sleep. He would, I would go to bed and maybe one o'clock, well, he'd go in the bathroom and he'd be in there until five o'clock. Readin'——

"The last time I went in the bathroom was about three - thirty. . . . I mean, so when I went in the bathroom he said, 'Nothing is wrong; everything's all right.' And he was rubbin' his chest like this (demonstrates to interviewer). And I said, 'What's the matter, you got pains?' He said, 'Ohh, I have pains all over.' And I says, 'Oh, what's the matter?' He says, 'Oh, nothin', go back to bed, I'll be all right.' Then I went to bed. And I must have went into a deep sleep. Because the next thing I knew I heard the bell, it was about ten minutes of six. And he must have left the house——not too long, after I went to bed. Uh - huh, 'cause I was up, oh, the last about ten days quite a bit, 'cause he was, uh—he was always rubbin' his chest, you know. I don't know what it was from. I, he didn't go to the doctor because he told me he would NEVER go back in the hospital again. And I told him he didn't have to go, you know? He didn't have to go in the hospital. And they came and they told me. And that was it." (SULLIVAN 4.III.14)

Mrs. Burke reviewed the events as follows:

"Now I should have known that something was wrong, he was starting to get depressed like in January. The night before I heard him go down in the basement, which he never does, he hated to go down in the basement. I would wash the clothes down there, he would be waiting at the outside door and we would hang up the clothes. But he

would never, never go down there. But that night he was
down there, and I went down to see what he was doing,
and he had torn all, almost all the photographs from our
trip to Bermuda five years ago. I can't remember really
how long. But when I saw that, I just cried, and said, 'The
only thing I have now are my memories, and you're destroying even those.' He looked at me, but he didn't say
anything, just walked upstairs and went into his room and
shut the door.

"Later that night he tried to put his arms around me, I
guess to console me, but for the last year he couldn't
rightly show affection. We would go to kiss him, and he
would just put his head down, like this, and the kiss would
land on his forehead. He didn't seem to want anyone to go
near him, to touch him. But he didn't know how to give
affection anymore, and I guess he was trying to but didn't
know how when he tried to put his two arms around my
shoulder. I think he was destroying those photographs, and
then he tore one or two of them upstairs, 'cause he didn't
want to be reminded of when he was younger and still
well. Anyway, I should have known that something was
seriously wrong then.

"The next day as we left he asked me, 'Do you have the
extra key to the house?' We keep an extra key in the den.
And I should have suspected something then too, 'cuz he
would always let us in the house when we returned—we
didn't go out very much without him, but Joan had to get
away sometimes and I would sometimes take her out for a
drive, and if he refused to come, well——

"Then I got to the car, and I said to the kids, 'I think I
forgot to kiss Daddy goodbye.' I went to the door,
knocked, he let me in and I kissed him on the forehead,
and he seemed so happy, he gave me a great big smile. He
always used to have such a beautiful smile, everyone com-
mented on it. We were only gone two hours, such a short

time, when we got back and the door was locked and he
didn't come, and he wasn't sitting in his chair, I knew right
away something was wrong, something terrible. I ran right
down to the basement, I just felt I must, and————he
was already dead." (BURKE 2.1.6)

Mr. Burke had hung himself.

Initial Reactions

Mrs. Sullivan had what must be a very common response
aside from the shock—something "trivial" stuck in her
mind.

"He'd laugh. Then he'd say, 'You're going to live in a
pigpen when I die.' He always use to say that. That's the
only thing he criticized that I can remember. I use to go to
bed and I'd close my eyes and I say, 'Oh, I can't.' If he
ever stands at the bottom of that bed and says, 'I told you
you were gonna live in a pigpen.' That's the only thing
that stuck in my mind for the first couple of weeks." (SUL-
LIVAN 4.III.40)

Mrs. Sullivan was also in shock, and three months later
could only recall her anger, or "resentment," as she called
it.

"The most thing was the resentment, that's all. That's
the only thing I can remember. I never thought I could resent Father. I just figured he was sick and he didn't know
what he was doing, you know. You had to accept it that
way, but uh, now I don't accept that way at all. As a matter of fact when I can say, 'All right, Doc, I forgive you,'
then it will be the end of it. But I can't say it yet because I
don't." (SULLIVAN 3.II.42)

Like Mrs. Jefferson, Mrs. Burke discovered her husband's body and therefore also experienced severe shock.

"I keep remembering the bad things. . . . Every morning I wake up I think of that day. Every single morning. I feel so guilty. If only I hadn't gone out and left him alone . . . though he didn't know what he was doing at the time, of course. If he had, he never would have. He was a religious person." (BURKE 4.11.8)

Her trauma was such that:

Mrs. Burke, who made the funeral arrangements?

"You mean, who took over?"

Did someone take over?

"My daughter." (BURKE 8.v.19)

Ceremonies

"You may not have your father very long," Mrs. Sullivan had told their children more than twenty years earlier after he unexpectedly survived the operation following his accident. He was in the hospital eight times after that; she had expected him "to go" again and again. "Father may not be with us next Christmas," she told her children year after year. She nursed him then and cared for him for nearly a quarter of a century, and then he took his own life. Now she sat at a mass occasioned by her husband's suicide.

"Oh, yes, the mass was really very nice but you don't, you don't really know what's going on. You ain't really

sitting in that chair; you're a million miles away. You don't
know what's going on, you don't——I don't even know
half the people that come up there. I don't even remember——no, you don't——you're in another world.
You have to be, you know. I don't remember nothin'
really." (SULLIVAN 3.II.16)

In contrast to the services for the seven socially dying
who were previously discussed, the turnout was large for
both Mr. Sullivan and Mr. Burke. Family, friends, and
neighbors came to pay their last respects, and to comfort
these widows of men who were primarily unfortunate.

Subsequent Reactions While Searching

"I imagine that's what the bitterness is now. I imagine
eventually because I, I just, when Doc first, you know,
died I just figured well he was in so much pain that—I
couldn't feel sorry, I couldn't wish him to be alive. And
now I don't feel sorry for him. I think he should have
stayed and died the right way and it would have been better on the children. It's not a nice thing for the children to
remember that their father took their life, you know. It
isn't a nice remembrance of him and I resent it. Well
maybe that's the—the next step is forgiveness. I don't
know. I don't know what the next step will be."

You're resenting something that can't be changed.

"I know. That's what makes me madder. That's something that I can't do nothing about. I can't change it. I
know. I don't know, I couldn't tell you. It's just that, uh,
the way it is now I just resent him, immensely, and I never

thought I could. I resent what he did, not Doc, but what he did and how he did it, to leave that on the children's memories where they remember him as a nice man and a nice father. He was very good to them. He provided for them all and I don't like their last memory to be something that he committed suicide."

But that was only a very short moment. The rest of his life he led a good life, he was a good father, a good husband.

"But you think of the last moment more than you do the rest. I suppose eventually I will remember the others, I suppose. We got along very good. He spoiled me to a certain extent. I always had everything I ever asked for and I imagine in time I will think of all those other things, but right now I just think of what he did, and I guess it was a weakness or a cowardness or, I don't know. People say you have to have courage to do that. But I don't think it took courage to do that. You have to have courage to live, not to kill yourself. To me it's a weakness." (SULLIVAN 3.II.37–38)

After living with Doc, bearing his children, and being with him so much of every day, neither of them working, managing as best they could under the circumstances, Mary Sullivan certainly thought she knew her husband. When he behaved in a totally unexpected manner by committing suicide, her entire conception of her husband was challenged. After remembering their thousands of experiences together she inevitably asked: "Is this the same man who . . . ?"

Even as she looked at him at the funeral, she scrutinized his face for some answer.

"I don't know what I expected him to look like, I guess, I suppose, in the water, and I don't know what I expected him to look like, but I was quite surprised, uhh, that he looked just like he did. So I was very pleased, he looked just like he did. He didn't even look like he was dead. And I figured he'd have a—I guess I thought he'd have a frightened look or something on his—I don't know what I expected. But he didn't. He was very peaceful, very, very pleasant looking, and he didn't have the—I guess I figured jumping, or something, he'd have the—I don't know what I figured but I (sighs) he looked like he did when he was about twenty - eight, twenty - nine years old. They did a beautiful job on him."

Were you glad that you did bid the last farewell to your husband, actually see him?

"Oh, yes, because he looked very peaceful, very pleas-ant. Yes. It's what he wanted. He looked contented. He couldn't look that contented if it wasn't what he wanted." (SULLIVAN 12.x.20)

"I guess you really didn't expect him to die even though you talked about it, prepared about it, and then, ya never really expected it. Then when they're dead (not clear) I don't know, it's hard at first—the WAY he died—if he died in the bed or if he died when he was in the hospital or something, I don't know—maybe, uh, ya might have been more broody about it, I don't know. The WAY he died, it made ya mad, and I think that's—ya get over it faster. Madness, I think, works marvelous; it really does." (SULLIVAN 12.x.28)

From shock she went into anger, venting her feelings to herself late at night when everyone else was asleep. She began to lose weight, her already heavy smoking and coffee drinking doubled, and she suffered from insomnia.

"Every time I think of Father. . . . I'd get mad. . . . I just don't understand WHY?

"And I, the minute I'd walk in the house and look at the mattress and, and then I'd get mad and it's more resentment than anything else. I resent him. I'm mad.

"Yah. Yah. I never thought I would ever resent Father. How can you resent someone who's dead? (laughs) I never thought you'd—you figure he was dead, you'd never, but you do. And they don't even know you're doing it. Yup." (SULLIVAN 3.II.33)

Thinking of their life together she kept on trying to assimilate the fact of suicide into it. As a take - over manager she certainly thought she knew him.

"Yah, I'd——I knew that Father was in a mood and I didn't bother him about it until he got over it. Then, we would talk about it, but this one he didn't get over it. Like, he used to be in them a couple of days, then he'd go in them a couple of weeks, but then he'd get over them. But this one he was in for months and months, you know. I thought I knew Doc. I guess I didn't because I never thought he'd ever—I could read him; I knew when he was in pain by his face, the way he talked to me. I know in my household, and I'm the father [her words], which I suppose I shouldn't have done—I wouldn't let the kids bother him, and I guess I pampered him. I suppose I shouldn't have. But he didn't know I was because he wouldn't have stand for it (laughs) but I don't know; I must have done something wrong." (SULLIVAN 7.V.8)

Raised in the Catholic faith, she wondered about his Hell as well as her own.

"Well I think if he went to——church and to the priest and all, I KNOW that they say that, uh, the Church don't hold it against you any more, but I was brought up that if you took your life, you went to Hell. And, that (not clear) (laughs) and that's the way I was brought up and I cannot change my mind just because they now say that, you know—maybe in time I will, I don't know. But all my life——" (SULLIVAN 11.VIII.37)

The search went on and on. How could he have? Why? What did I do wrong? Mrs. Sullivan's search differed from some others primarily in that she did not fear going mad. She seemed quite convinced that "some day" she would sleep, she would eat, she would "forget about it."

"I just believe that human nature takes care of all that stuff. If it didn't, you know, everybody would be in the nut house." (SULLIVAN 4.III.44)

Mrs. Sullivan had family, including two sisters who had been widowed, one by war and the other from cancer. Consequently:

"Well, I just ask her how long it takes and she said about a year and a half. She says and then you wake up some morning and you're—she says 'I went three days without thinking about Joe and it dawned on me that I didn't think about him, and I almost died.' She said it takes about a year and a half. She used to cry herself to sleep every night, every single night. Her husband died very fast; he had cancer. He got sick in November and he was dead in March. And he was never sick, never, and he was dead and it was a shock like. She says it takes about a year and a half or two years she says and it dawns on you. You wake up some morning and you say, 'I went to bed and I went to sleep and I didn't cry, or I didn't think of Joe for a couple of days.' She says it does take a while and she looks different. She used to have that faraway look in her eyes all the time and now she looks like herelf again. Of course, I idolized her; I always did. Mmm, she was my older sister and she looks like Charity [younger sister] now. You know, she's completely different."

It took a long time for her to get back to herself?

"Mmm. She was married thirty - five years; that's a long time, you know, and they were—they were always together. They——" (SULLIVAN 3.II.31)

Such experienced support would be a powerful resource for anyone and Mrs. Sullivan both greatly utilized and benefited from it. That same family content, however, serves as a strong reminder of its missing member.

"These holidays, with Father gone. This Thanksgiving I should have stayed home. I went over to my son's—I was only there a couple hours and went back home again. I should have stayed home and did my own cooking. I always stayed home, and had them at my house. Seemed funny to have Thanksgiving with nothing to do—I should have never gone over. I guess it was that I had nothin' to do—so Christmas I'll stay here—I was pretty good until Thanksgiving, but four or five days after that, I didn't want to talk to anybody—Charity said Christmas is worse—I wish Christmas was all over—at least I'll be busy." (SULLIVAN 5.IV.1)

Mrs. Sullivan's subsequent reactions to her husband's suicide were thus anger and a private search for some reason why. She was able to search, to get mad in the late hours of the night in large part because she had no pressing responsibilities. Eventually she would have to go to work, but at the moment few demands were made on her.

By contrast, Mrs. Burke had the extremely pressing responsibilities of small children, plus an older one who needed special care.

"Well, remember I said that I went away for six weeks? (*Yes.*) I don't think I felt anything all summer long, I was in a state of shock, nothing hit me. I went away, and I had my family with me and I was so busy, I really enjoyed myself. Then when I got back, it hit me. I don't think there's ever a day goes by that I don't think about him. And with the children, often we get into, well, arguments, and before they wouldn't do this. And I always felt so much for the children, and then, afterwards, I realized that it's your husband that really comes first, that should come first. You can't depend on your children, like many people do, but when it comes to it, there is no one like your husband. . . . 'Cuz anytime the children do something wrong that goes against me, I start to think about him. They fly up against me, they never did when their father was here. They say things to hurt me, you know, and that's when I think about him. He would never have allowed them to talk to me that way——" (BURKE 12.VII.6

"The guest speaker at last month's sodality was a priest who is a marriage guidance counselor. He talked about how frequently opposites attract each other, and I thought about how different Don and I had been. He did everything for me, I really depended on him. He was a stickler with the children—like they'd be out ice-skating over at the pond and he told them they had to be home at five, and they'd be five minutes late, he'd really give it to them. He couldn't realize that it takes a few minutes to get off the ice, to take off your skates, put your coat on and walk home. I don't care if the kids are a little late—they stay out at least a half hour later now, like Sonny has hockey practice. I don't mind it." (BURKE 4.II.5)

The Burkes were seemingly quite happily married for the twenty - five years before his stroke. He apparently needed obedience, not care during this period. Consequently it is only after his stroke that they conform to the syndrome found among most of our widows. Nevertheless, in that one - year period care was needed, managed by take-over and unsuccessful.

When stress is placed on any living thing, even in transplanting a plant for example, a period of dormancy seems essential for later growth, if not for survival itself. Mrs. Burke had the trauma of her husband's stroke to contend with at the same time that she had to take over everything, including reading the newspaper to him. Her already strained resources were further drained by her daughter's now worsening congenital heart problem and its accompanying retardation. Then she returned one day to find that her husband had hung himself in the cellar.

The demands upon Mrs. Burke were such that she truly had no time to mourn.

Could you describe the second month—after you got back?

"Well, that was mid - August, and then I went away again—see, I kept going away, I went to New Jersey. I really didn't stay home at all during the summer. I think I felt I didn't want to stay home. And then I went to New Jersey, things to keep me busy. Yes, because when you're busy, you don't have time to think." (BURKE 12.VII.9)

Mrs. Burke thus did not involve herself in any search for an explanation, avoided the entire subject of death, and thought others around her were doing the same.

How did you find out that others knew the circumstances of death?

"Oh, just by talking to them. When people don't ask questions you know they know." (BURKE 8.v.9)

Mrs. Sullivan had quite the opposite reaction.

"Like, I had to change my beneficiary on my policy. I tried to talk to William [son] about it but he didn't want to talk nothing about it. 'I don't want to know nothing about it' and he wouldn't talk about it. I says, 'You've got to talk about it' and I told him about it and I guess maybe it was too soon. I don't know; I should have waited. Maybe it was too soon after Father had gone (not clear) to think of me, you know."

Have you done this yet?

"Oh, yah, I changed it last week. My other nephew is an insurance man and he changed it for me. But I did change it. I figured I'd be terrible if I didn't, you know, and if something did happen you'd have to wait a year or so, you know. My nephew called me up and asked if I was thinking of changing it and I said 'yup.' I says, 'I just didn't get around to asking you to bring home the papers.' He brought them home the weekend and I changed it; I put William's name on it. He's the head of the house in here now. My other three are married." (SULLIVAN 3.ii.35)

This experiential period we are calling *subsequent reactions* had another feature that deserves attention before moving on. Recall that half of the wives practiced the mutual deception game involved in the taking - over style of husband management, foremost among them Mrs. Sullivan. She and the others made sure that their husbands never found out about certain things, and there were also things she did not tell others about her husband. Two of the seven previously discussed widows had taken over their husbands (Mrs. Zack and Mrs. Codman), but both had broken this pattern by their withdrawal. Mrs. Sullivan, however, practiced mutual deception to the end. Because they were deceived by her in the past, others now quite logically suspect that the widow is again withholding information.

"In the last couple of weeks she's [daughter] been talking about Father and she never done it before. She wanted to know if he left me a note and I didn't tell her. And I says, 'No,' if he did I would show her. She says, 'I don't think you would. He might have said something that you didn't want us to see.' I says, 'No.' I don't think she believed me. But he never did." (SULLIVAN 7.v.39)

Mrs. Sullivan was, of course, not the only one seeking an explanation. Her children and the other members of the family also both wanted to know "Why?" and felt that they had to work out some sort of satisfactory explanation. So Mrs. Sullivan had to deal with even these suspicions.

Reinvolvement

Due in part to others' questions, and even more because of the need to deal with the problems those questions raised, Mrs. Sullivan was forced out of her isolation. Not that she was physically alone much of the time.

Do you see much of her [her son's girlfriend]?

"They live up my house (laughs). They're up here all the time. . . . Bill and Liz figure I shouldn't be left alone. So they . . . I have more girl friends (laughs) and stuff in the house than I can stand but I feel well, if it makes them feel better by doing it, I'll let them do it. They'll get over it after a while." (SULLIVAN 7.v.30)

She began to react to others' reactions to Doc's death, seeing their problems and helping them to adjust, and helping herself in the process.

"And I think, Joan at first resented me being alive even though she doesn't know it, I think that's what she did. Because, uh, she, uh, she wouldn't even come over here for three or four days at a time and she NEVER missed a day coming in my house. But now, she's back to normal again. I guess she's accepted his death and before she wouldn't do it. And I think, at first, she blamed herself 'cuz she got married. Because it seemed that she got married and then Father killed himself. And at first she thought, 'That's why he did it.' And oh, I just yelled and screamed at her. To think that my, all my married life, and he did that because she got married? (laughs) No. So I straightened her out and now she's all right." (SULLIVAN 10.vii.9)

From this point she moved on to deal with other problems as well.

Do you think they're grooming you for a possible re-marriage?

"Oh, the oldest had a fit. I, if I get mad on Liz I'll say, 'I'm gonna start goin' out.' 'You can't. You're married to my father.' 'I mean your father is dead.' 'That don't make any difference, you're still married to my father.' Oh, I think they'd have a fit. Absolutely! And then Liz said to me, 'You're too old' (laughs)." (SULLIVAN 8.VI.1)

She had gotten "mad on Father for what he did," saying at the same time that she knew she got mad to keep from going mad. Although she had talked to her deceased mother, through prayer, asking her "to help me to bear" Doc's misfortune, she would not "talk" to Doc because she was mad at him. "He should have stayed and died the right way." Getting mad did work for her apparently, as evidenced by this "communication" from him seven months after his death.

Yes. Tell me, how's the Bingo going? Had any wins?

"I won twenty dollars last Thursday (laughs). So I can go for two more weeks (laughs). I haven't won too much since Father died. But I used to win every week and then, uh, but I started, the week before I won ten dollars and maybe Father's forgiven me that I'm mad at him (laughs)." (SULLIVAN 7.V.33)

By the eighth and tenth months she began to feel the release that death also sometimes brings.

"I was married and had someone boss me all my life and I'm my own boss now and I ain't gonna give it up for anybody else (laughter). That's MY—(laughs) MY attitude. I think when you're married, you give in an awful lot to your husband. You keep peace in the family, stop arguments, you more or less bend to his ways. And you pretend all the time. Now, I don't have to pretend. There's a contentment——I don't know what you call it—but

I'm enjoyin' it. And I ain't giving it up for somebody else (laughs). I can go out, I can do what I want, I can come in when I want, I don't have to . . ." (SULLIVAN 8.VI.7)

"———I'm getting use to being by myself. And I don't RESENT it like I did. I guess I'm getting over it. It takes time———it's a matter of time. But I'd never marry again. In a million years (laughs). ·I guess I'm myself now. Marriage is a lot of pretending, I guess. Uh, I'm finding out myself because I haven't had it in thirty‑one years, thirty‑two years. I guess I'm enjoying this freedom. I don't know (slight laugh). It's funny after not having it for a long time. (*Yes*.) You know? And I guess I'm like a little kid (laughs). I can DO and go and say what I want to say to do and go and say. And I don't have to think that it will upset Doc. And that just came up the last couple of weeks, I guess. And it's, uh———and I get guilty. For feeling that way (laughs). You know? Crazy (not clear)." (SULLIVAN 10.VII.12)

The critical importance of context in understanding death as well as life is evident especially with these two widows, who both expected the death of their husbands but had never expected it to be by suicide. One got angry, engaged in her own search, then returned to the world of the living. The other would neither express nor search, largely because she could not, such were life's circumstances as she found them. Mrs. Burke thus experienced no reentry because she had never been able to leave.

A Year from THAT Day

What is unresolved within us does not simply disappear, as Freud so brilliantly perceived over a half century ago. Instead it seeks an outlet elsewhere, there to defy solution until its twisted course is retraced. Without family or financial resources, and at the same time with an on - going daily need to utilize whatever was available, which was mainly herself, Mrs. Burke understandably transferred her panicked emotions to her care-needing daughter.

"The heart doctor sees what's happening, and turns on me, he says it's all my fault. He tried to tell me that I had hostility toward her, and he got me all upset that day. I do so much for her, I turn myself inside out, and he tried to tell me that I felt hostility toward her. He thinks that I shouldn't be taking care of her, shouldn't be with her any more. But like today, I don't even know if she's taken her heart pills. I have to remind her. No one else would do that for her." (BURKE 12.vii.3)

Given Mrs. Burke's coping pattern of transfer from husband to daughter, most of her communication to us revolved around that daughter. Rarely could she talk about him at all. We set out to do research, but accepted from the outset the possibility of the need to secure professional care for our volunteers. On three specific occasions we put Mrs. Burke in touch with services she needed. She requested this help from us, but being concerned for her and her family, we also in part solicited her request.

Unfortunately, the same pattern we observed much earlier among our other widows now proved true for Mrs. Burke. She was The Caregiver. She would accept no outside help. Just as Mrs. Banks in the middle years of her marriage to George would seek no help, the prognosis here was not good.

When asked to review the previous year with us, she could only skip that year entirely and jump back another year to when her husband had suffered his stroke, saying that he had really "passed away, for me" at that time.

When he could no longer be the strict husband and father
he had been for twenty - five years, Mrs. Burke had had to
become a new person, and that, after all, was what each
woman had to become after the death of her conjugant.
Truly Mrs. Burke had been forced into this process twice
in the course of a single year, first when what he *was* died,
and then when what little was left took that, too. How
many of us could now face the prospect of yet a third
death?

As the year ended for Mrs. Sullivan, she documented the
phases we have already been through, then added another
dimension.

"Well, when I first heard it was a SHOCK . . . it was loss.
Then it was——MADNESS, and madness stayed a long
time. I was mad. And I think even now sometimes I still
get mad." (*Yes*.) "When I hear other people talking about
they're going here with their husband, they're going there
—you still get mad." (*Uh - huh*.) "And I think, the longer
it is——the more you realize how alone you are. At
first, after you get over the madness and everything, it's
uhh, your FREEDOM—it's a, it's a nice——contentment. It's a nice feeling to have no one tell you
what to do, at all, you know, especially if you haven't
done it for such a LONG time. Then, as, uhh, times goes by
a little bit, it's, uh, it's a lonely feeling. Right now it's just
LONELY to think the rest of your life, you're gonna be by
yourself. It's just a lonely feeling. I mean, you hear the
others talking about their husbands, they're going here for
their vacations, they're going there for the weekend—
(*Yes*.) There's nothing to plan for, there's nothing to come
home to. It's such a lonely feeling." (SULLIVAN 12.x.13)

A year from THAT day she visited his grave for the first
time, but did not yet feel herself adjusted to his death by
suicide.

Did you have a memorial mass for him?

"No, the kids didn't want it—Elizabeth and William didn't want it, so I says, 'No, we'll wait. Maybe next year we'll be more adjusted to it.' " (SULLIVAN 12.x.10)

Summary

Two women started to become widows while their husbands were still alive, for they knew death was soon to come. One had cared for her husband for nearly a quarter century, the other for about a year. Even as their husbands were deciding on suicide they continued the care, while knowing he was not to be with them long. Somewhat like the women on the way to the divorce court, they were headed for widowhood from death by natural causes, when the hands of their husbands intervened. Now they were what they had soon expected to be, but through a different route.

After the shock, anger boiled up in one, the other could not even afford that. So one searched to answer why, the other just went away. Life after death continued into that path worn by the life before it, the one to finally accept life as she found it, the other to avoid it and fixate on something else.

THE STRANGERS TO DEATH

In the nine cases we have looked at in this part, the husbands could be said to have reached the beginning of the end before death ended it all. These cases stand in sharp contrast to the three women from whom we will now hear.

The three strangers to death had married men who

needed care from the outset. Like the other widows, they gave their care; it came to occupy the central portion of their life space, and was maintained at a constantly increasing cost. Although these three were earlier included among those on "The Downward Spiral," an important qualification is now germane.

At the time of the descent, all twelve men deteriorated socially and/or physically. Willing social death, seven women began to distance themselves from their husbands. Another two, knowing natural death was at hand, also began to emotionally prepare themselves for life without their husbands. By contrast, for these three women alone there was no evidence of the slightest withdrawal.

Mr. Sloat had, in fact, slashed his wrists six weeks earlier—in despair, he said, over being unable to provide for their new baby. An epileptic, he had been fired after having had a seizure at work, in spite of his good work record, and could not find another job because of his condition. The attempt had been directly confronted, and all felt everything was "okay again." This attempt notwithstanding, Mrs. Sloat felt good about the future and, perhaps even more importantly, she felt she had a future with her husband.

The future also looked bright for the Tibbetts. They had the initial papers to adopt his three sons from a previous marriage, were comfortably enjoying a wide circle of friends. They had just had a good time at a veterans' convention they always attended. Pat had not drunk too much this year, partly because Mrs. Tibbetts kept him on the dance floor—this annual reunion of former World War II prisoner - of - war - camp comrades had been an especial success.

Mr. Ago had been caught selling heroin and sent to prison. Although this had broken up the house playing that we witnessed earlier, both saw it as probably good. Mr.

Ago had been forced off junk, was in better health these three months later, and in fact was now excited about learning a trade. Mrs. Ago visited him twice weekly as permitted, promised to wait the remaining fifteen months of his expected eighteen - month actual term, and remained living with his parents.

Their Penultimate Communication on THAT Day

"Well, see, when I left in the morning it was already ten minutes of eight which I knew was late for work and he was dressed in chinos. . . . He hadn't worked for a couple months becuz, you know, he had to stay out of work in order to be qualified, to be able to qualify for medical retirement from the state. And so he always got up and we had coffee and he, he ate breakfast. So, uh, I wasn't a big breakfast eater, but with him, I had to, so we had breakfast together and uh, we had discussed what we're, what we're gonna have for supper. . . . And when I came back at noontime, of course, the boy had found him flat on his face, heading for the refrigerator, instant coffee on the stove and the, the teakettle going. Yah, the teakettle. Well, you know, whatever you call that thing." (*Sure.*) "So apparently he was, he was in the process of making a cup of coffee and he had a cigarette in his mouth, and he fell flat on his face, and that's when he died." (TIBBETTS 13.xi.14)

Mrs. Tibbetts was summoned home from work by her stepson, who found his father when he came home for lunch. "The police asked him if he thought his father took his life. And this upset him so that he didn't even stay around. You know, he left the house." According to Mrs. Tibbetts the police then went upstairs and searched through the bathroom medicine cabinet and their bedroom dresser, taking with them several bottles of the medicines he had been using for the last twenty years. A neighboring physician then arrived (about the same time as Mrs. Tibbetts), "to pronounce him," tentatively ruling the death due to a coronary. Ten days later Mrs. Tibbetts received the official death certificate and the information that the medical examiner had ruled the death to be by suicide.

Although there was no delay in ruling the death to be by suicide for Mr. Sloat, the medical examiner's finding was vigorously contested in this case, also.

"Tommy didn't kill himself. He was sick, he had epilepsy and that's what he died of, an attack. The doc wouldn't listen, he just wrote down 'suicide' on the death certificate, he didn't believe me when I told him." [She then opened up a carefully folded piece of paper that was lying on the table. It was a photocopy of the death certificate.] "They sent me this, look, it don't have nothing about how his head was hurt. . . . Six weeks before he died, Tommy tried to kill himself. Took the razor and gashed both wrists. I found him and he was bleedin' and I brought him to the hospital and they sewed him up. So the doc just knew he tried to kill himself and wouldn't belief he didn't do it this time. He couldna' done it. He had the radio on, by the bathtub. And the coffee pot was goin'. And the letter was lyin' in the next room, he started it, to his brothers. He said how glad he was that he was gonna see them soon. Would the radio be on if someone was gonna kill himself?

"I found him when I got up, he was lyin' with his head sorta bent down under his arm, in the water. I pulled the plug out, and the police, two police screamed at me, why did you touch anything on the scene of death? And he'd banged his head, he had a seizure. But the doc wouldn't belief it, said he couldn't see nothing. See, on the death certificate there's nothin' down under 'injury'? How am I gonna tell my kid that he didn't kill himself when it's written down here?" (SLOAT 2.1.2)

The night before Mr. Ago was to be transferred to another institution at his own request, he was found dead by the prison authorities. They insisted it was suicide and we have their word for it.

Initial Reactions

"When I first heard he was dead, I was shocked, I just couldn't believe it. The priest . . . [after introducing himself and identifying the wife] he says, 'Well, he just committed suicide.' So I said, 'Who are you kidding? Get out of here.' And I slammed the door in his face. 'You're a liar. Get out.' " (AGO 14.VI.4)

"Well, the first month I used to wake up at night, screaming for my husband. Because, how I know that, my brother and them was staying with me, and they'd wake up hearing me yelling—that was when I was at the other house—and I always say it was a blessing, in a way, that that house burned up. Because if I had lived there, I probably would have done something drastic, or would have ——'cause every time I went into the bathroom I could see him in the bathtub . . ." (SLOAT 13.VII.14)

Mrs. Tibbetts began by saying, "You know, when you lose someone like this it's like a big chunk of yourself, you know?" She then went on to talk of how she felt "kind of sorry for myself," and also felt guilty. "What the heck did I do wrong and why was I such a nag, and what could I have done to be a better person." When she turned to the label of suicide that had been decreed some ten days later, her reaction was one of pure anger, but *not* toward her husband.

"The one that pronounced him made no qualms about saying that it was a coronary at the time, he made no qualms about it at all. . . . And, uh, and even at the time when the coroner came to the funeral, uh, he made no qualms about it. And then, uh, when the diagnosis was changed, it got me really completly upset. But, uh, uhh, I don't know, I just think that, uh, they're not feeling— they're not feeling people, that they, they feel very little empathy for people." (Tibbetts 14.xii.7)

"See the doctor that came knew that he had been a prisoner of war and that their life expectancy was much shorter than other human beings. You know, right now it's about seventy, but with POWs it's about fifty, fifty - five, alright? And here he was forty - eight . . ."

I'm sorry to keep coming back to this but what I don't understand is why the doctor didn't make the assumption that it was an aneurysm or some other form of a death from a circulatory failure.

"Well, I, as I said, I questioned him. I said, 'You know, it's, it's—in Massachusetts it's, it's a state law that if you find a person dead and he hasn't been treated previously for an, any particular, uh, illness, it's, it's mandatory that you do an autopsy.' I said, 'Why didn't you do one on him?' He said, 'Well, you know, if I was to do one on every one, I'd be doing two hundred a week.' So then I got real mad and I said, 'Well, what the hell do you think you're being paid for?' I said, 'If you can't do that job. . . . If you can't do your—you know, if you can't do it, then you shouldn't accept the job.' But I said, 'I think you're doing, you've done this man a big dis—a big, uh, disfavor,' and I says, 'and the family in particular,' I says, 'now we're going to have to live with this the rest of our lives.' " (TIBBETTS 13.XI.11–12)

Regardless of any truth in Mrs. Tibbetts's contention —reserving that exploration for later—here it will suffice to point out that "truth" is what is said on paper. This is the "truth" to which the widow must react. It is the "truth" about which her friends will hear and in terms of which they will console her. And it is especially the "truth" of which statistics are made. Because the doctor certified that the cause of death for Patrick Tibbetts was suicide, that is what it is.

This Official Reality is further supported by psychiatric reality. These three women were just beginning life with their husbands when they confronted death, and they surely did not want to believe it. Death caught them unprepared and suicide was even further from their reality. That he was dead they wished to deny with everything that was in them. That he himself was responsible just simply could not be true. He was dead—that they had to admit. So their anger focused on the closest contestable thing, namely, the manner and means by which death had come about.

Denial, angry denial—for their husbands could not be the target of their anger. Instead it was directed outwardly, against the doctors and the police, the medical examiners and the undertakers, against anyone other than the man death had robbed them of. To be bereaved means literally to be "robbed," "stripped," or "dispossessed." "All joy was bereft me," forcibly taken away.

The seven women who had invited their husbands to die in their lives were not robbed. Neither were the two to whom death came with only an unexpected face. For these three women alone can it truly be said that they were bereaved. And thus it is only with them that bereavement follows its classic pattern.

Here, then, are three initial reactions to unexpected death by suicide, three cases of numbing shock mixed with total disbelief and intense anger.

"The first time I met Dr. Wallace I was really numb and I blabbed on and on," Mrs. Tibbetts told us six months later. The emotions they felt were of such intensity that they could not permit themselves to feel anything. Before flight there is that period of absolute immobility, that reactive dormancy necessary for survival. Early in life we learn that feelings are necessary for survival; that the pain of fire, for example, keeps us away from it. Ceasing all activity, including remembering, likewise can help one to survive. Later, each widow had her own response to her husband's death by suicide, even as she had her own response to his life. But at this first moment these three women all shared the shock.

They were therefore understandably vague in telling us how they initially felt. They were numb when we talked to them two months later, and could not tell us how they felt either then or earlier. As Mrs. Tibbetts put it, they "blabbed on and on." It was not until two, three, even eight interviews later that they could talk about those first few weeks. Nor did we ask them. We sought to understand each woman individually, and hear what she wished to tell us. She told us her story and we listened, asking questions relevant to what she was then saying. Fourteen months after the death we did ask a series of questions of the "Where were you born?" variety, but in the first twelve months after the suicide we primarily just listened.

Although our several relationships to these widows is described in detail later, this explanation is necessary so that the reader will understand that the widows are not now talking about their initial reactions at the time they had them. They felt the loss, the broken heart, the anger, the guilt, and the rejection initially, but could only tell us about those feelings much later, if at all. In addition, the critical reader should know that later their feelings changed, as did their memory of what they felt before.

It was at this point that we researchers entered their lives, and this explains in part their intense communication to us. In the first interview, after a few minutes of introduction, they spewed forth the feelings they had felt forced to hold within, teaching us immediately of the isolation they had experienced. We listened as they talked. As we listened their chances of survival increased; in this lies a lesson for us all.

Ceremonies

The Tibbetts had just left their veteran friends on Sunday, and on Wednesday Mrs. Tibbetts alone greeted these same friends. The neighboring doctor who had pronounced Patrick Tibbetts dead by coronory thrombosis was there, along with the small town's medical examiner who would shortly rule otherwise. His family, her family, and her still unadopted stepchildren were there. Some arrived early to take over the house, make it ready for the wake and friends' visits, and to comfort the bereaved. Shocked silence prevailed.

Included in the company was the author of a book about his and his fellow soldiers' experiences in the Japanese prison - of - war camp, where death had claimed so many, where so few lived until their "Reprieve from Hell," as he called it. "Pat's life," he reflected, "had been one hell after another until this second marriage." Now Mrs. Tibbetts would enter hers.

Mrs. Ago went to the florist with her mother to select the flowers that were to be put on display at the wake. Because she and her husband both liked "simple things," she selected "a small bouquet of daisies and a little ceramic poodle vase. My mother's eyebrows raised up and so did the florist's but they didn't say anything to me." She took two of the daisies out of the vase and placed them in the coffin on the third day of the wake, and pressed two more in a religious scapular her husband had worn around his neck. She has the vase, the scapular, and the flowers in her room to look at whenever she thinks of him.

Although Mrs. Ago complained about the length of the wake, she was pleased that so many people came.

The priest who had married the Sloats and who was giving instructions to Mr. Sloat for his conversion also read the funeral service that was held at the undertaker's parlor. The undertaker was a friend of Mrs. Sloat's mother, and he made most of the arrangements, including picking out the clothes and putting the notices in the paper. He endeared himself to Mrs. Sloat by telling the newspaper that Mr. Sloat died by drowning, a story the priest also apparently believed long enough to bury Mr. Sloat in consecrated ground. Later he reportedly said that had he known, he would not have done so.

There was also a wake and these services were attended by both families plus a number of friends. It was in the style of the poverty class, but no less loving for that.

These three ceremonies thus stand in distinct contrast to the nine others. There had not been nor was there now any attempt by the wives to distance themselves from their husbands. All three deeply felt their loss, were numbed by it, and knew that their husbands could not possibly have committed suicide. And no one insisted otherwise.

Subsequent Reactions

Shock lasted longer for these three widows than for the others, and its shift into anything else was far more subtle. Perhaps it would be most accurate to say that whereas the initial period was unmitigated shock, with an infusion of other - directed anger and total disbelief, the subsequent period was one of repeated "freezing and thawing." Tentatively they asked themselves, "What if he did?" (They couldn't say *suicide* yet, but always referred to it obliquely.) They searched briefly for an explanation, then retreated into the sanctuary of shock, feeling numb again.

"I used to carry on bad, after he died, every few days I'd carry on, and my Ma said, I was up to her place 'till late that night, she said, 'Okay, you leave him [the baby] here tonight.' And I was asleep, in my bed, and I saw his face [her husband's] in front of me in my dream, and he was like he was sayin', 'You come along, come along with me.' Then my girl friend who lived downstairs was shakin' me and said, 'Get up, the house is on fire.' I ran down, grabbed two of her kids, ran back, grabbed the other kid and we stood out front and just watched it . . ."

Do you think your husband was trying to contact you? Where do you think he meant you to go by saying "Come along"? Did he mean you to come where he is now?

"Oh, I think he was there, from heaven, it was God's Will that he died and he tried to save me. No, he didn't want me to die too, he wanted me to walk out of that fire, to be saved." (SLOAT 2.1.4)

"I get that feeling often. Well, some nights when I get home I feel that he will come home, and I expect to find him in there, but I come in and I don't see him here. Then there's times that I think that he'll be comin' home and I leave the door unlocked and I wait for him to come home. Then I get up at about two o'clock and lock the door. Like the times I will say to him, I'll say to his picture, 'Can't you come back?' or somethin' like that, and afterwards I say to myself, 'I must be goin' crazy or something.' " (SLOAT 4.II.20)

Mrs. Tibbetts also feared that she would really "go crazy."

"The first month I was numb, you know, I was really in a fog. . . . The second month I was feeling kind of sorry for myself and feeling, starting to feel guilty. I felt we were really pretty close. So, we had our spits, but you know, spits and spats, but I didn't really feel that, uh, a rip - roaring thing. I mean, uh, the biggest, the hardest thing I ever threw was a pillow, you know, a toss pillow. But, uh, it's been magnified to the point where I felt so guilty that I was—this was when I felt, by the third month I was going insane, really, you know, and this is when I called the psychologist. . . . And this is when I really flipped, I really blew the top, and, uh, I told him that I was all screwed up. My head was spinning like a top and I had not slept for three months, really slept, you know, you'd doze and I said, 'Jesus, I'm so full of guilt feelings it's pathetic.' And I said 'I don't know how to get over them.' " (TIBBETTS 6.VI.29,30)

Two of these three women contemplated suicide during this time.

"If I hadn't had this talk with the doctor, I think I would have handled it much differently——and perhaps ruined everything. At that time I really contemplated suicide for about three weeks. I don't know how, because I don't have the courage——although I still think of it. About the third month I got very depressed, and I couldn't put my finger on it, really, except I, I was going through the motions, I was gettin' crankier around here——I was sort of avoiding everybody, which I knew was not right. And yet I didn't know how to get over it. In the meantime I felt like I wanted to die——more and more. You know, I said, 'That's kind of stupid too. I don't have the guts'—and by this time my head was really spinning. I couldn't sleep nights. I really hadn't slept for about three months. He said 'Do you take sleeping pills?' I said 'No, I don't take sleeping pills.' He said 'Why not?' " (TIBBETTS 5.v.2)

". . . when I was at the other house— . . . everytime I went into the bathroom I could see him. . . . And one night I said, well——I was always takin' my bath in my mother's house, and this one night I said, well I'm going to take it in my own house. Like I wanted to see what happened——and I fell asleep in the bathtub that night. And my brother . . . kept pounding on the door and I finally woke up." (SLOAT 13.vii.14)

Shock has brought them through what they perhaps could not have otherwise survived. Being angry and not believing in the death nor in its cause by suicide also played a role in survival. Contemplating suicide themselves helped them to understand in part what their husbands may have felt and thus they better understood them. All of these feelings were difficult to bear; yet it must also be remembered that they were and are basic survival reactions.

There is a wisdom of the body; not a mystical force but the balancing of systems for survival. To feel was unbearable so they did not feel; to think was not possible so they found themselves a million miles away. The impulse to survival is present throughout; its manifestations merely change and now become more consciously directed. The interviewer reported:

"She said that she didn't allow herself to think about what she was doing. She said that she has to do this quite frequently and that this is really her formula for coping with the death. She said that every time that she thinks about her husband she ceases the activity or inactivity at the moment when she's thinking of him, therefore, no longer thinks about him. She said that it would be too upsetting if she allowed herself to dwell on the memories.

"She told me that she is now sleeping better than she did, feeling much less nervous than she did, and has been able to 'talk herself into a better frame of mind.' Her mother told her as a child that one can talk oneself into doing almost anything. When she goes to bed at night, she almost hypnotizes herself into going to sleep by thinking of tranquilizing scenes like sunsets or peaceful pastoral views that she has seen. It is effective and she falls asleep almost at once.

"She is taking fewer tranquilizers. She takes tranquilizers now only about twice a week when she really feels that she needs them. She finds, however, that she rarely needs them with the intensity that she felt that she did a month ago. She has made concerted efforts to be less nervous in the same way that she has been talking herself into going to sleep at night. She uses positive thinking and thinks about a peaceful state of mind if she feels herself beginning to shake and she said that it is almost immediately effective." (AGO 5.II.4)

"The second month . . . I found that I was feeling a lot sorrier for myself and, ah, this is when I did more crying. The third month I still did crying but, uh, in the crying and, and I think the feeling changed from, uh, well the second month in addition into kinda talking to myself I was getting angry at, uh, at everything, really. You know, somebody uh, kept needling me about something that was, to me was unimportant, or not that important, put it this way, I would get extremely provoked which wasn't usually my nature." (*Yes*.) "Uh——some of the—a few people I worked with, one nurse in particular, God, she has no, uh, will, she didn't have much empathy anyways. But she kept needling me something terrible. She drove me wild. And so that, after the second month, well, it was, as I was feeling sorry, I became extremely angry at her. I was very angry at the church——I was angry with, uh, well, you know that, that Jack was angry at the, at the (unclear) at the town here. Then it changed. The anger continued but then I also started getting depressed, really depressed to the point where I thought of taking my life. And this went from, I would say from about the third month to the seventh. And I really thought about it. I thought about it almost every minute." (TIBBETTS 12.X.3)

For at least half the year she withdrew from social life, avoiding even those close friends of theirs they had left at the veterans' convention on Sunday only to see them again for Pat's funeral on Wednesday.

"Do I see couples? No."

Did you have special friends that you used to do things with?

"Uh, not particularly. I seen a couple, but, really—to be honest with you—I seen them too soon afterward, you know."

Do you think you avoid seeing them now?

"(Crying.) I know I do. I know I do because I feel that once everything is under control—you know—I get better control—and yet they are awfully nice people —you know I'm not saying I don't like them. These are the ones that Pat thought a great deal of. As far as his relatives, well, I go to see them (sniffing), I try to see his mother often, once a week or so, she's elderly, and she thought a great deal of Pat." (TIBBETS 3.III.43)

The suicidal feelings passed and Mrs. Tibbetts turned her attention to her stepchildren, whom she adopted after asking them if they wanted to go back to their mother. They said No. Even the nineteen year old who was then in the Army said that he wanted to be part of his stepmother's household. She had her problems raising three nearly adult boys, but she found she could express her love for her husband through his children, and they gained a home away from their alcoholic mother.

"He's not dead, he can't be. He couldn't have killed himself, he wasn't that kind of . . ." Shock, anger, sadness, depression and disbelief, the contemplation of suicide and the fear of insanity—these are some of these widows' reactions to deviant death. Unthinkable thoughts; unshareable feelings.

Reinvolvement

From a conscious effort to survive, we began to observe the widow's beginning perception of others' reactions to the deviant death, finding in the fact of such perception a surge to survival. Earlier they were locked within themselves, children's demands notwithstanding. Now they began to see those around them.

Any questions from Jimmy [her son]?

"Not a bit. ——Uh——he doesn't ask a thing. As I said, he's, he does a lot of uh—he's pretty quiet and I think he's still tryin' to live in a world of fantasy. Or the, uh, yeah, fantasy. I guess that's the word, because he—— all, uh, it has a lot to do with the uh, a lot of programs he wishes to see, uh, the, uh. 'Dark Shadows,' for instance, you know spooky things. The uh, things that are unexpected, or uh, the unreal, uh, well, it may not be unreal. Maybe ten years or fifteen years or twenty years it may be real, but this is what he, you know, programs that pertain to, uh, like, like I like to watch David Susskind, to be honest with you, on Saturdays, you know. Many controversial problems, you know, such as——if there's not a good movie I like to watch him. But I, really I don't like to watch even a movie——I'm not interested in them. You know? I haven't (not clear), I enjoy David Susskind but this type of thing, he dislikes. Because it's dealing with the here and now and he can't do that——or he is unwilling, let's put it that way. Can't, I hardly, I'm not one to say he can't or he can, uh, it's just that he doesn't want to. He'd rather watch, um, like I say, things that to me are, uh, monsters, you know. If, if it's anything grotesque and monsterlike, well, this is what he enjoys. This is what he pre-

fers watching. And this is why I say, let it just, uh . . ."
(TIBBETTS 8.VII.23)

"I thought at that time that I've got to start making
changes within the house so that the memories aren't always, you know, the memories—I'll always have memories but, umm, they won't be as painful." (TIBBETTS
6.VI.41)

Mrs. Tibbetts then started redoing first one room and
then another in her house, signaling the change within her.
    Mrs. Ago moved back home.

"I was feeling a whole lot better because I was back
with my own family. They were the best thing in the
world for me. My brother, the one that's in Worchester,
you know?—he used to ask me every single night if I
wanted to come with him and his friends. Every night he'd
ask me—we're very close, we always were before, he'd
come and see me several nights every week when I was
married. ——Then there was my best friend, the one
who had the house at the Cape, remember?—well, she'd
come over all the time and I'd go down there every weekend.

"Well, the whole summer I just went down to the Cape
every weekend, I was feeling real good because I was back
with my friends, not Bobbie's friends any more. And they
are very nice people, people I've known all through high
school, all through school. You know how it is to be with
your friends—I would say there were a few bad days,
but it seemed that every day I got a little better.

"Um, it was all right in September, I guess. For the fall,
I was just mostly working and coming home. I'd go out
shopping with my mother—she'd say well, 'Joan, I've
got to get something or other, or there's a sale on, come on

out,' and we'd go out. My mother was wonderful, she
knew what it was like, she'd been through it herself.
'You've got to keep busy, busy, that's the only thing for
it.' " (AGO 14.VI.6)

"Now it was Christmas when things started to go bad.
Christmas made me feel real bad, it brought back memories
of being with Bobbie on Christmas. See, my mother had a
lot of people, a whole lot of people over for Christmas, I
know it was on my account, she made it as good as can be,
but I did feel bad—and got more and more depressed
after that. Then my car all the time wouldn't start, and I
would say that started everything bad—this lasted for,
let's see, a month and a half."

What happened, if anything, to change this mood?

"I met Gene [in the tenth month], and ever since everything has gone all right! [Gene did not know the circumstances of the death, nor that Bobbie was in prison, nor
that he was an addict.] In Bermuda I told him the whole
story for the first time. He was a little shocked—he's
been through a lot himself.

"Where I went through the death of my father, it prepared me for death. I could face Bobbie's death better.
That helped, and my family around—it was terribly
hard when my dad died, I thought I would never get over
it."

Have you?

"Well, I guess not really, but I mean that real pain and
crying every day. But I knew what I had to go through
with Bobbie, and it was easier for me, knowing I just had
to wait it through . . ."

Can you tell me any differences in getting over the two deaths?

"Well, the first death, you think 'How does anyone ever live with this?'—but I think Bobbie's was a little bit harder, because I felt older and more self - conscious of people. You know, the way he died, I felt a little queasy. I think everybody at work knows. I never told anyone he was in jail even, Bobbie made me promise not to, he said it would hurt me in the long run, so I didn't tell them about that or—how he died. So, to this day, I don't know to this day, they never said anything about it. But I know that some of them must have read about it. My girl friend at work knows, but she wouldn't say anything about it. My mother told her about it, she thought someone should know what I was going through, you know, to be able to understand or something. She told her to keep it a secret from everyone at work, so she told the others he died from some sort of an accident. But no one ever has said a word about it.

[Gene is the only person she has told about the suicide, jail, and drug addiction.] "It's made us even closer. I never thought of telling anybody—but Gene was telling me about his stepmother, and we were sitting on the beach and he said, 'Why don't you tell me something about you?' I think he was hinting around, he wanted me to tell him about my being married."

Had he heard about the suicide? Any indications?

"Absolutely not. He didn't know anything before—he had heard he had died and that was it." (AGO 14.VI.7–10)

Mrs. Sloat began to see her friends again. She said that some of her friends wanted to pretend that Tommy never existed and wanted her to go on and live as if he had never been. She said that she did not feel that was right, that she could not do that. When asked how she thought it ought to be, she replied: "I don't know but you just can't forget him. He did exist. He did live and I guess you have to live knowing that." (SLOAT 5.III.14). Undoubtedly, Mrs. Sloat's reentry was incomplete at this time, as it was later.

A Year From THAT Day

If you look back over this past year, can you tell me how you feel now compared to just after the death, and give me a description of how your feelings changed over the year?

"Well, I survived it——"

Are you surprised?

"Yeah, I really am, when I remember how it was all at one time there, I'm really surprised I got through it. I thought the way everything was happening there for awhile I was gonna—go—crazy. Everything was all happening at one time. But now—I figure what comes —part of the, uh—well, I think what keeps me goin' is my son! Now, I keep saying I gotta bring him up." (SLOAT 13.VII.9)

Her son and supportive family greatly helped her to survive, but her primary tactic for survival remained that of denial.

Through the final interview she insisted that Tom did not commit suicide. Her first explanation, possibly true, that he had a seizure while bathing gave way to other explanations that bordered on the bizarre—that he'd been murdered by his brother, for example.

Unable to sustain any of her several explanations, Mrs. Sloat delved into numerology. The conflict between her number cycle and her husband's became the reason for his death. She also communicated with him through dreams, asking him if he really did kill himself, seeing a judge punish him for abandoning his child, saving her from the burning house by his timely dream warning. Lower class in background, living on and off welfare, undernourished and unattractive, her chances of marriage were slim before Tom and less promising afterward. Thus in the particular context of her life, she lost much.

Initially we attempted to calibrate separate behaviors such as grief reactions, and then favored holistic analysis, which was more parsimonious with our design. We also concluded that items such as visits to the grave could not be interpreted out of a life's context. Mrs. Sloat's grief reaction, however, would be rated as severe by almost any reckoning. She visited her husband's grave from eighty to one hundred times during the year, screamed for her husband night and day for months afterwards, and as the following indicates, probably still could not believe that he was gone a year later.

Well, tell me. How did the anniversary day pass?

"Well, I went to the cemetery, to the grave. And I cried some. I could imagine him——"

How did you get there?

"I walked. After my brother said he wouldn't take me I figured he wouldn't go near there, so the baby and I went up——"

How did you spend the rest of the day?

"Well, I went over to my girl friend's for awhile. And she remembered what day that was, and she was pretty shook up." (*Was this Naomi?*) "Uh - huh. She got pretty shook up over it. When I went home that night, I went over here and I couldn't stay here, I had to go back to my mother's. I just couldn't——"

How did you feel that next day?

"Oh, I was all right the next day. Yup. I had no—— (crying softly)" (SLOAT 13.VII.9)

How often about do you visit the grave?

"Every three weeks. 'Cuz my brother figured out that was the most safest time for me to go, 'cuz the way I was doing, every other week, he said that was too much on me, he could see it."

Did it upset you?

"I used to cry every time I went up there. And now, it still bothers me when I go up there, but he says I'm not getting myself upset so many times. He sez, the other way it was twice a month, now it's just once a month or twice every other month. He sez so it doesn't have that much effect."

Does it work out better for you?

"Yeah. But he figures, like last Sunday I was supposed to go, and I sez to him, 'Are we leavin' at the same time?' And he said 'Not today.' So then I asked him today about tomorrow, and he said 'No, next Sunday.' See, he figures that tomorrow will be the twenty - first, that'll be a year, by the date—and it is best for me to stay away!"

What are you going to do?

"I could get there on foot if I wanted to, but he won't approve of that very much, and he won't—he'll say— 'You want to go on foot, you go on foot.' "

What do you think you'll do then?

"I'll just take a walk with the baby in the morning then. 'Cuz if he sez no, I go by what he sez. On some things. I think he knows what he's talking about."

Do you think you might regret not going?

"No. Because he's got the idea, he told me, 'Marg, you go up there'—well, I was telling him that I was gonna dig up the grave. I always say that." (*Good heavens!*) "And he got the idea in his head that if I went there tomorrow, I'll dig the grave up, and he doesn't want me to dig the grave up."

Why do you say that to him?

"Well, I've been thinkin' since the day my husband died, or since the day he was buried, that how do I know he's really dead? Because when they say he's bleeding in the funeral parlor, I start thinkin' and I say I never heard of anyone bleeding in a funeral parlor. There might be some blood in him, he might even be still bleedin'. But they don't know. They said 'Marg—they say he's dead, he's dead.' I said yeah, but there's not everything they know. They haven't found everything today."

Would you really consider doing that?

"I had thought about it. I went as far as thinking the shovel I used to shovel the snow this year—it's a good shovel for digging the grave. But uh, now I say well, it's too long now—it wasn't then, if he wasn't dead then he'd be definitely dead now. He'd be all bones, might even be worse——" (SLOAT 12.VI.31–33)

Denial, bordering "on the edge," no doubt. It is also denial pressed into the service of maintaining integration.

"I'm feeling differently. Oh, I don't know. I still have his picture under my pillow——but it's, uh, it's getting to the point where you, you've always—it may sound cruel—but you almost forget how they looked, until I look at the picture. That's the way it is—with me." (TIBBETTS 12.x.41)

Mrs. Tibbets had come a long way on the path to survival when we talked to her a year from THAT day. She was even proud of her own progress.

"Well, I mean, I don't mean this to be conceited but I think that I'm acting out a lot less, let's put it this way." (*Yes.*) "And we, I don't overreact like I used to. I used to —really, you know, a little molehill was really, hey! they were going to get it two barrels. But now really, you know, I, I, feel that I can stop and, and, evaluate the situation and, uh, respond to it as I think it is necessary. You know, if, if, if it doesn't re——if it's not really that important, I don't feel that I have to respond too dramatically to any situation, any given situation——whether it's at work or here [home] you know?" (TIBBETTS 12.x.22)

She had gone back to the church with which she was very angry earlier, attending with the boys on the day their father died, then visiting his grave. Her life had begun to have a more positive outlook.

Do you think about the next year? Do you look forward to it?

"Yah, I, uh, I look forward to next May. ——Crazy! No, I, uh, I, uh, no I look forward to it, really, not just next May. I think because, uh, you know, as time goes on I'll have more freedom." (*Yes*.) "Not that I—I'm not the—I've always been sort of an independent individual anyways. I've had to be. And then, and then, when I got married, there was a little bit of difficulty to give it up and I sort of liked it. And I think this is one of the things I resented with having to take over all the decisions again." (TIBBETTS 12.x.23)

Mrs. Tibbetts's main problem continued to be "what it said on the death certificate." She worked in a Veterans Administration hospital as a nurse and so she was familiar with required medical procedures as well as with suicide itself.

"There was one fellow from the psychiatric ward who had privileges, and he made, he was so intent on committing suicide that he planted a seven - foot iron fence, walked up the telephone, that was a high tension pole, and he latched on to the wires. Well, naturally, he fried. You know? He stayed there until he just dropped. And so it was very obvious what he was gonna do. So then there was a great big investigation. This is how the VA operates. All of a sudden they're all concerned.about suicide. You know, so they say, 'Well, the guy doesn't have the right to take his own life if he wants to.' You know. Well, this again, is, is almost like, uh, euthanasia, really. In a sense, I suppose. I don't know. ——You know, I, I'm talkin' like uh, I'm pretty liberal - minded, but when it comes down to my own feelings about what has happened to me, I think, uh, I haven't accepted what was on the paper. I don't believe it. And that's it. I don't belive it."

Do you think you're rationalizing?

"Do I think I'm rationalizing? Now? No."

Avoiding it?

"Avoiding what? What's on the paper?"

Denying it?

"Uh——"

I mean, what are your feelings on this?

"My feelings, well, it's there, I can't change it. Right?" (*Uh - hum.*) "I have to accept, I mean, it's there, I can't change it, but I don't have to believe it." (*Uh - hum.*) "And I don't belive it." (*Uh - hum.*) "You know, when, when we first started talking?" (*Uh - hum.*) "I had a lot of anger for feelings. I had a lot of guilt feelings! I had a lot of, uh——you know, I, I had feelings which——well, maybe, Jesus, I was, maybe I was a nag. Maybe I was a bitch. I don't know. You know, what female isn't at times?" (*Uh - hum.*) "But you know, when I talked with Jack [stepson], he said, 'Jesus, you know, you, you're nothing like what Mom was. You know?' At that time nothing had happened. I mean, I hadn't adopted them. And

I said, well, you know, I do, I do overreact at times, but uh (not clear), I don't know. But now I don't think I'm rationalizing at all at this point. I suppose now your next question would be, 'What would I say if somebody asked what he died from?' ——Oh, you're a dog (laughs slightly). Wait a minute. What would I say? 'A heart attack.' ——And I say this and I really believe it. At this point." (TIBBETTS 8.VII.32,33)

Tell me something Mrs. Tibbetts, would you feel better if you knew one way or the other?

"Oh, absolutely, absolutely. I think I said this to Dr. Wallace. Uh, you know, uh, I know I have faults. I'm a bitch sometimes, you know. I can be a nag, too, just like everyone else and, uh——you know, I think if I'd known that, if, if, uh, I had known for sure that this is what he really did, well, maybe I'd feel a lot guiltier, too. But by the same token, I think that maybe I could grow, in this respect, in learning to be much more tolerant with people. And try to understand other people a lot better. But had it been, you know, uh, if, uh, if the autopsy had shown it was a heart condition, well, I knew his life expectancy wasn't this long and, you know, again, I, I would have spoke, perhaps felt bitter and angry because I lost him this quickly. But, uh, I think I would have felt much different in either case. One case I couldn't 've done a thing about, the other one, if I missed the boat, and he was depressed and he did die from an OD then I think, uh, I would've done my darndest to try to become a better person and, and, uh, not that I, not that I've stopped but, uh, you know I think I would have perhaps maybe gone overboard a little bit perhaps. I don't know. But I, I think I would've been a lot more tolerant. We've had many lectures on suicides since that one and I've attended every one of them, boy, and I'm telling you I listen like, uh, there's no tomorrow, you know, because I uh, I try to, uh, see, try to understand what people are really thinking. We've been lectured a whole week on suicides from, uh, doctors from California. You know, is it right and is it wrong? And the moral values and everything else. But, uh, yes, I think I really would feel different—one way or the other." (TIBBETTS 13.XI.13)

A year later these were Mrs. Ago's reflections.

"It all seems like just a dream, like a bad dream. I've blanked out most of it in my mind, all the things I didn't want to face—even the terrible things of my marriage —things I wanted to blank out from it—well, I managed to do that. ——He was a great person, really. It was just the drugs that brought him down. . . . I don't think I am building him in mind what he wasn't. If you could have seen him when he was off drugs, he was a completely different person, really wonderful. He was kind, so sweet and thoughtful to me, always thinking of me then. When he got back on drugs it was like a—a business with him, all he could think of was where his next fix was coming from. I can honestly say this—he preferred heroin to me.

"When they told me I didn't even cry. I thought it was the end of the world, but I couldn't do anything, couldn't speak. I just stood there. See, I'd just talked to Bobbie, and every time I came he said 'Everything's going to be okay. I'm going to kick by the time I'm out, I'll be all right again and I'll have a trade—you'll see, everything will be fine.' " (AGO 14.VI.4–5)

Mrs. Ago was in shock, then angry with the prison authorities, then blocked any further questioning from her mind. It's hard not to know the answer, but the answer may be even worse. Fearing this, she said she preferred not knowing. She said after some discussion of the possible mode of his death that she really didn't want to find out at this time how he did die. The reason that she did not want to find out was not only that it would hurt her family ("they're all I have in this world"), but also that she didn't feel ready to face this information. She feels that she may in time, but meanwhile she prefers wondering instead (Ago 5.II.6). When asked if she had observed the anniversary of Bobbie's death, she replied:

"That was funny. His mother called me up—it was on a Saturday that I went to say a mass, I mean go to mass, I didn't have a mass said for him, then I went over to his grave, I put flowers on his grave and just stood there very quietly for awhile looking down at the grave—I didn't cry. —But his mother was so stupid, imagine this, she didn't even observe his death, she called the next day and said she called the church too late to arrange for a mass, or something dumb like that.

"You know, I felt when I was there [at the grave] that he is better off where he is than where he'd be right now if he was alive. He'd ruined his whole body with it [heroin] and he'd be in prison, right now—and I don't think he could stand to be alive if he were." (Ago 14.VI.3)

After playing house with her junkie husband for a year and a half in his parents' home, she moved back to her own home, there to be again looked after by others. When things came back to the surface she diverted her attention in another heterosexual attachment, and thus was able to survive largely through repression. Often the word *repression* is taken to have an extremely negative connotation, but that is not intended here. Within the limits of her life's circumstances, Mrs. Ago was able to survive, to accept the second traumatic death in her experience, and a year later her life did have forward movement. As always one should be extremely reluctant to judge another—understanding others is both more difficult as well as (mutually) more rewarding.

Summary

Three strangers to death unexpectedly became instantly acquainted with it. Unlike the seven who were withdrawing from their husbands, these three desired no separation. Unlike the two who expected death but not suicide, these three women expected neither. Whereas nine of the women had some social and psychological preparation for widowhood, three had no such anticipatory socialization. They alone were truly bereaved, robbed, dispossessed.

Not one of the three would or perhaps could believe that her husband chose to leave her. Being forced to adjust to a totally different present and future was already too much for them to bear. So they all denied the suicide, and one even tried to deny the death itself.

Disbelief and shock were both more intense and longer lasting in these three widows than in the other nine. Anger was also present and expressed with considerable force, but again in contrast to the other nine, it was never directed against the husband. He could not have been responsible, they knew, so the anger they felt found its outlet against the church, the doctors, and the police, against anything but him.

Rarely did their search for an explanation give rise to an examination of their husbands, again in contrast to what we learned from the other nine. If it was not an epileptic seizure it must have been murder, Mrs. Sloat in effect said; and if not that, then the mysteries of numerology contained the answer. Their search thus differed from that conducted by the other nine in that it probed the external features of their husbands' lives, seeking explanations from without rather than from within.

All three of these widows had reasonable grounds for their disbelief that it was suicide. How could anyone commit suicide in prison, drown himself in his tub, or die from barbituate ingestion in less than three hours? These doubts notwithstanding, the medical examiners had ruled suicide, and so that was what it was, however strongly they might deny it.

Denial pressed into the service of maintaining integration, for all three of these women feared for themselves. Two of the three contemplated suicide and also feared that they would go crazy, even with denial. Denying his responsibility for their loss enabled them to survive when they felt that their very survival was in doubt.

Reinvolvement came more slowly to these three women than to the other nine, and their denial of the suicide persisted through the end of our year's contact with them. Two said they would not consider remarriage, but the third was actively involved with another man. And they were no longer strangers to death.

OTHERS REACT

THE STORY of these twelve women is not yet complete, for just as their reactions to their husbands' extended relationships that in turn influenced them, so others' reactions also had a powerful influence on them. The reactions of the officials connected with these deaths must also be observed if we are to understand the social context of their bereavement.

FAMILY AND FRIENDS

Four of the twelve women had no family nearby for consolation and support; two of them, Mrs. Miller and Mrs. Burke, had no close friends either. Two others (Mrs. Jefferson and Mrs. Tibbetts), had family nearby but neither sought nor received any close emotional support from them, but one of them had friends at work. Three of twelve widows were thus forced to survive without help from family or friends. Mr. Burke's former employer did help the family on several occasions, Mrs. Jefferson's friends on the West Coast did help her on her single weekend visit with them, and Mrs. Miller did have the support of "the girls" at work; yet none of these sources was constant or close. The other nine women were more fortunate. Eight had two or more friends or family members with whom to talk, and the ninth had one.

The value of these family and friendship relationships should not be underestimated. These women were in need, and their family and friends could respond to that need. Remember that few of these women had ever sought outside help for themselves or their husbands, and that now there was the additional stigma of suicide to inhibit them from seeking help.

Have you had any feelings of stigma from outsiders or people in your group of friends or acquaintances?

"Of the ones who know?—Have I got any pains of stigma? No, I think, I think they've accepted it, uh, you know, the whole situation. Right from the beginning I think these people, uh, the ones that I did tell it to, have accepted it and they've accepted me so that I don't feel this. But, they're, you know, as I've said before, there were still a couple who I never would tell. Never speak of it, you know, for those reasons." (TIBBETTS 13.XI.22)

They were thus cautious in approaching others, yet needed someone with whom to talk.

"Everything is fine one minute, then just awful the next. . . . Sometimes I just lie there and wait for the morning, and I'm so glad when the morning arrives. Uh, initially back in March occasionally I would call my sister up. But you can't pull that one too often at 2:00 A.M. She was understanding, but I knew that would have to cease (laughs)." (CODMAN 8.IV.10)

While there are many ways in which we might describe a friend, perhaps we would all at least agree that he and/or she is someone who will listen to you when you want to talk.

"They don't talk too much about Doc dying and how I'm feeling, how I'm getting over it. They just say, 'You look good Sis.' That's all. And then we talk about other things. That's all. We don't talk too much about Doc. They figure, if I want to talk about Doc, I'll talk about him." (SULLIVAN 10.VII.8)

Nine had friends and family who would listen, and who also knew when *not* to listen.

"They called me and I said, 'No, I don't want to go.' And Fran [daughter] said, 'You've GOT to go.' She says, 'You've got to go.' So, she says, 'If you're with them you won't be talking about it.' Because I, I—that's all I did. I mean I must have gotten on everybody's nerves, you know. I'd say, well, gee whiz, why did—' you know, well, it was just—it was just—stupid, you know, the way I, the way I was carrying on. Uhh, so I did go out and they took me out and we had a drink and I felt better, I felt a lot, a lot better. And I really—I had a nice evening, you know." (BANKS 12.VII.38)

Friends *know*.

"She made a few recommendations about getting rid of his clothes and she said, 'Knowing you I bet you didn't get

rid of everything.' I said, 'Shut up. You're right.' " (TIB-
BETTS 6.VI.23)

Knowing, friends could say things to the widow that no
one else could.

"Ben didn't know Clyde was dead, so, you know, he
plunked down beside me and he said, 'Where's your husband?' And I said, 'He's dead.' And he goes, 'How'd he
die?' I go, 'He killed himself and I got $10,000 for it.' And
he goes, 'That figures, you killed him for his money,' and
he made a joke out of it (laughs). This stumped me, you
know, it was so beautiful (laughs) and he says, 'Who's
your next victim?'

Excuse me?

" 'Who's your next victim?' Yah. I needed that. Hah!"
(JEFFERSON 6.III.39)

It is hard to imagine anyone else serving the widow as
well as her friends did, when she had them. First of all they
listened; if they had not done so, their other aid would
have been for naught. Then they alternately protected and
pushed, changed the subject and got the widow busy, according to what they thought their friend needed. When
present, such support was a powerful ally in survival.

It is tragic that all of the women did not have such good
friends, and that the support that even some of the nine
had was not all that most of us would desire. Some friends,
for example, pretended that the husband had not died,
while others pretended that he had never lived. The needs
of some friends even victimized the widow herself, when,
for example, they insisted on working out an explanation
for themselves in spite of the sensitivities of the bereaved.

Just at the moment that the widow needed their accepting embrace, they had to have their questions answered. They might be seen as of the same ilk as those friends who think that feelings are not to be felt, communicated, recognized, understood.

You can go ahead and say what you feel.

"Well, yes, because when you talk to your family the first reaction you get, 'Oh, you shouldn't feel like that.' You know. Well, this bit 'You shouldn't feel——' How can you help feel this way? And unless they've experienced the same feelings, you know, why do they say that you've got no right to feel this way?" (TIBBETTS 12.x.42)

Told that they should not, often must not, feel "that way," the widow had no alternative other than to withdraw further into herself, feel more outcast, rejected, alone, and hurt. Forbidden thoughts, forbidden feelings, left alone to find their own way out, no wonder four of the twelve contemplated suicide and one even attempted it. Possibly some of the twelve husbands were pushed down their route by a similar unsupportive social fabric.

HEALTH CARE PROFESSIONALS

At the professional level, the twelve suiciding husbands had all been in contact with a number of health care professionals. Only Mr. Banks and Mr. Jefferson could be said to have escaped the attention of our society's treatment, therapy, counseling, and psychiatric programs. Yet for all this contact, the care received was inadequate and ineffective.

Continuing their husbands' experiences, the twelve women fared little better. Mrs. Codman stated that several weeks "afterwards" she had gone to see her husband's psychiatrist.

To what effect?

"Not that I learned anything, he said pretty much what I thought he would, what maybe he had to. He felt badly about losing a patient."

Mrs. Codman did not think that the psychiatrist was fully sensitive to his own situation, the situation of her husband in his life, and wondered quite sincerely what good he thought he had done for her husband (CODMAN 3.i.26).
In addition to the foregoing report, Mrs. Codman got a prescription for tranquilizers for eight months from her family physician. Lay practice not unexpectedly followed suit.

"You should've seen the people that offered me tranquilizers at the wake, you wouldn't believe it. I'd just take them and put them down in the ladies' room. I had millions of them. I swear everybody in the world's on tranquilizers." (SULLIVAN 3.ii.12)

The twelve women did find a path to survival but it was not often due to concerned health care professionals. The twelve women had few who would listen to them, few who were able to respond to their life's struggle. In the original outline of this manuscript, an entire section was tentatively entitled "Caregivers." This section was to report on those who aided the widow on her path to survival. As I went through the one hundred and four interviews, this section was dropped for want of sufficient instances. Some family members and friends did listen to

the widows, but most did not. Neither did the professionals with whom these women were in contact.

THE OFFICIALS

The officials were even worse. The police violated the pri-
vacy of Mrs. Tibbetts's home and the sensibilities of their
thirteen - year - old son in asking him if his father killed
himself. With one exception the funeral directors exploited
the widows in their grief; frequently they were able to collect their money directly from agencies such as the Veteran's Administration or Social Security. The nearly desti-
tute Mrs. Banks paid eight hundred and seventy - five
dollars for a "modern" mortician to take her husband's
body to the crematory. If she had not gone there in a family car, her bill would have been even higher. This mortician had been highly recommended by the city morgue.
She paid for the cremation and urn for the ashes in addition. "He took me," she later realized.

"This is really a money - making proposition. See they
got you at a moment where you're most vulnerable to anything. I mean here you've lost someone that you cared
about and you want to feel that you're doing all the right
things and you want the best for them, naturally, and,
uhm, you're kind of confused and caught up in all this.
. . . He sat at his desk and he said to me, did I want to
have in the paper, uhh, oh, my husband's schooling and all
this and I said 'Yes' because I knew this was something that
my husband was very proud of. . . . And when I got all
through, that little tribute that was in the paper cost something like seventy dollars, and in comparing notes with this
friend of mine who had lost her husband, she said, 'Why I

just called the paper and told them the same thing myself.' " (GRENON 3.II.17)

"But then they immediately went about calling the undertaker, in spite of the fact that I have an uncle who's an undertaker, I wasn't consulted. You see, there are two undertakers in town but I wasn't consulted as to which one I wanted."

Who did the calling?

"The police naturally. Uh, you know there's a lot of footsies. They play together—if you call this one here, you get a little bit of payoff." (TIBBETTS 6.VI.5)

For ten months Mrs. Grenon received telephone calls from the "monument people," "calling me about when am I going to put a monument on his grave. 'You MUST get a marker on BEFORE THE GROUND GETS SO HARD that we CAN'T put anything on it.' " These calls came as late at night as ten o'clock even after she became "really furious."

The police illegally collect "evidence" to "solve" the crime of suicide in the dead man's home while the mortician investigates what life insurance policies are in force. This was the widows' usual experience with the authorities. The medical examiners then made their contribution.

Their work is not pleasant, nor are their professional reputations usually aspiring. Paid in most counties throughout Massachusetts by fee from the state, their appointment is at times political. Reexamine the twelve findings they made in their service to the state. Pat Tibbetts had lost forty - five pounds in the six months preceding his death and was in extremely poor health anyway. While I avoided launching a private study of cause of death determinations, nevertheless I remain convinced that Tibbetts

did not commit suicide by intentional barbiturate ingestion.

Ask your own medical authority if it was possible for
Mr. Sloat to drown himself in his bath. Turning to Mr.
Ago, have you even wondered why prisons have so many
"suicides"? A finding of murder would require willingly
testifying witnesses after a successful investigation. A ruling of negligent or even accidental death would be equally
difficult. This is the undeniable context of the official word
to us that Mr. Ago did hang himself the night before his requested transfer elsewhere.

"Acute depression while walking the MBTA tracks" is
the fourth of these findings that many may question. Unless he can communicate with the dead, the coroner had no
basis to judge the psychological state of the deceased. The
sole medical examiner I did interview told me he hadn't
"made a mistake in twenty years. Oh, of course, some people have objected to my rulings, but I just tell them if they
don't like it they can take it to court. It's an open, a public
courtroom but if they want everybody to go into it, that's
their right." In twenty years, several had contested this
medical examiner's rulings, he told me, in spite of its public
nature, but in only one case had he been overruled. That
was because the judge had been bought off, he explained.

Arrogance and incompetence exist in all quarters and
people do make mistakes in applying labels, even in life and
death matters. Still, four questionable cases in twelve is a
poor record.

"When they came up with this stuff, you know, I says,
'Jesus, if, if you're gonna put it down on paper, in writing,
at least prove it—by doing what you're supposed to be
doing. Not just by blood work alone.' I don't think that
this is the answer, or law. This could apply to any disease,
you know. You can do a blood count on someone and if

they've got a high white blood count, which means that
they have an infection, it doesn't mean, it doesn't mean
that they have appendicitis. It could mean anything. You
have to do other things, you know, it's just like in your research. You just can't take one, one meeting and, and write
up a whole paper on it and assume that this is how all people react. It has to be many things. And I think that they
were remiss in some of their duties. And I resent this. I still
resent it but, you know, so I still resent it but I'm not
gonna do anything about it. It's, it's over and done with.
I'll do the best I can with life and that's it." (TIBBETTS
12.x.35)

Obviously it is essential that cause of death be established, but special proof of suicide might be required as it is
for murder. The suicide's survivors might have a legally
protected right to give their testimony.

The objectives of the law as well as those of medical research could be reached without making cause of death
public information, as is now done. The information regarding cause might be given only to the "next of kin" for
dissemination as they think best. There are the young and
the aged, even the town gossips to be protected. Increased
accuracy in determination, confidentiality in application
—these measures would alleviate some of the widow's suffering.

THE CRIME OF SUICIDE

Beyond the administrative changes just mentioned, the greater problem may lie in the basic concept of suicide itself. First, what is the "crime" of suicide? According to the esteemed legal scholar, formerly an associate of mine, Helen Silving, suicide arose as a crime in English and in Roman law to prevent tax evasion!

"The crimes for which the Roman and English suicides atoned were capital crimes—in early Roman law, mostly homicide. Since after the suicide's death, the homicide could no longer be established, it was deemed at law never to have occurred. Thus, by his act, the suicide eliminated the homicide from the record, in a sense, substituting suicide for homicide. This later led to the definition of suicide as murder." (Silving, p.85)

By suicide, a man accused of a capital crime could save his estate for his heirs, as forfeiture could not take place until judgment was rendered. "Hence the frequency of suicides in cases of conviction and the introduction into the law of a rebuttable presumption that suicide implies confession of the crime charged, carrying with it—in the absence of rebuttal—confiscation of property" (SILVING, p.81).

It is thus from the state that suicide arose as a crime, for the Bible contains no prohibition of suicide, and the early Christians even exalted suicide under certain conditions, as in defense of virtue. The earlier confiscation of property that the suicide sought to avoid was never part of the American experience, yet suicide remained a crime or at least a "grave public wrong" (New York Penal Law § 2301, 1944).

Why? Who is protected by the prohibition against suicide? It cannot be said to protect the ostensible victim, for the perpetrator and the victim are one in the case of suicide. Nor can any threat of punishment be held to deter the person intent on suicide. Laws against attempting suicide, in fact, merely punish those who are unsuccessful at it. Clearly our law and moral injunctions cannot protect the suicide from his own hands.

Whom does the law making suicide a crime protect? A psychiatrist colleague insisted that it was ourselves we were so concerned about. Without legal, social, and moral injunctions against suicide, we would all do it! Were *that* the only thing that keeps us from the bridge, or gun, or pill, or whatever, perhaps we had just as well.

A less debased view of human beings might see the origin of the crime for America in the citizen's ever-constant attempt to outwit the state. When charged with one of the several hundred offences that carried the death penalty in the lands our immigrants came from, by conviction of which the state seized all property, who would *not* end his life a few months earlier to preserve his heirs? Many obviously would and did, so the state perpetuated its first injustice by a second, making suicide sufficient presumption of guilt for the crime charged.

This is the historical context of the crime of suicide in the United States. Although today suicide and its attempt is a crime in only a very few states, and prosecution is rarely instituted, moral censure is nevertheless widespread. Whatever its origin or statutory status, many of us still apparently feel it is totally reprehensible.

To fail in a suicide attempt is all too often to be sentenced to prison - hospital. Apparently we feel that listening to a crime—worse still, listening to someone's involvement in a crime—must be a criminal thing to do. So we lock up the would - be suicide in prison - hospitals, and lock those connected with the crime out of our lives. The would - be suicide must survive, we say, but he and his survivors must survive alone.

In spite of numerous excellent studies (see Bibliography), we also continue to stereotype suicide. Suicide is not a single, unitary event with little variation. Like the life that preceded the death, suicide has many different reasons.

You mentioned that you could read his face to see if he was in pain. Do you think he was in more pain?

"At the end, yah, all the time. He used to sit and rub here continually, all the time, he'd rub his chest."

So it was his chest actually that was paining him?

"I don't know if it was his chest or if that was just a habit he got at the end, or something, but he did that at the last, ooooh, four months. Yah. And if I'd catch him, he'd stop. Like if I'd watch him and he'd catch me watching, he'd stop."

Did you ever ask him why he did that?

"A habit. He'd say, 'Oh, that's just a habit.' But he never did it before."

Did you ask him if he hurt there?

"Yah. He said No." (SULLIVAN 7.v.10)

How many active working men would accept life incapacitation and its near total dependency? After six or seven years of hospitals and operations, who would willingly submit again? Mr. Sullivan chose not to enter a hospital ever again; he wished to decide the circumstances of his death. I have no answer, but persist in thinking that there must be an easier way out for people like him. And are pills and the bottle all that our society has to offer those who defended us in time of war? The years from age eighteen to twenty - two in a concentration camp, from twenty - two to twenty - five in a military hospital, this was the price Mr. Tibbetts paid, this was the human cost of war long after even the generals had faded away. The end of his suffering becomes the occasion for the suffering of those he loved. These bureaucratic machinations appear to be the random, unintentional cruelty of the system to which we all contribute.

The alcoholics had been committing suicide inch by inch for fifteen or twenty years before taking the final step. Was their suicide comparable to that of the young student, Mr. Zack? Once again some change in the very concept of suicide may be in order.

How do you feel about somebody committing suicide?

"I think for some people it's the only way. I think for him it's the only way, if he did it. You know. Because there just wasn't anybody that he could really, that he liked, really. He did say he loved me. In his own strange way, he did. But I don't think he liked me (laughs). There wasn't really anyone that he liked. He was just anti-everything. And I don't think there was anyplace, he used to talk about pitching a tent somewhere way out, you know. And I think this would be about the only way that he could exist. If he could do this. Just live alone, live away from everybody." (BANKS 10.v.40)

I know this is a very hard thing to think about, but if your husband had died from a natural cuase, can you possibly imagine how you would feel now?

"Yah, I think it would have been accepted very easy. But he was supposed to die for years and the doctor told me I was lucky that he even lived as long as he did live, and the kids knew. I used to always tell them your father, this might be your father's last Christmas, it might be your father's last birthday. It would have been expected because they always knew it. But not this way—not at all this way" (SULLIVAN 3.II.40)

Suicide cannot be accepted because we don't accept it, regardless of the circumstances, even when the very fact of suicide is doubtful.

The prison officials told Mrs. Ago that he had died of strangulation, of hanging. "But they changed their story twice, once they said he did it with his pants——imagine that——then they said it was a towel——but how on earth could anyone kill themselves that way?" Mrs. Ago believes that he had taken drugs. "You know they have drugs all over that place, I know that for an absolute fact. I asked the warden if he hadn't gotten hold of some drugs and he said 'We don't have drugs in this place.'" It has crossed her mind that her husband may have been murdered by one of the other immates. She said that once when she visited her husband he told her that one of the guys had been murdered. None of the inmates would tell the warden who had actually killed the boy, so it went on record as an accidental death. The reason that no one told the warden was that "They were scared for their own lives, because, you know, the one that did it would probably kill them too if they talked." (Ago 4.1.4,5)

Suicide arose as a crime to prevent citizens from depriving the state of its booty. The Church aided that effort until we all came to believe that no one had the right to end his own life. Hume, Montesquieu, Beccaria, and Fichte have argued to the contrary. And to Schopenhauer, "No human right is more incontestible than man's right over his own person and his own life, and if he does not wish to live for his own benefit, it is exaggeration to require him to continue living as mere machine for the benefit of others" (Silving, p.84). Silving herself believes that "the 'personality' rights of man include the right to dispose of his own life." (Silving, p. 91)

"Really, that man was so good, heart of gold. I think he done that most [because] he can see himself go. He was —he knows in a little while he would be in a mental hospital. Or he give us trouble, and he didn't want to give trouble to anybody. And I think most he done that so he wouldn't give me any trouble. He told himself, 'I give her enough trouble, I don't want to give her any more trouble.'" (Morneau 15.ix.3)

"And who's to say what's best for a person? It's not a very popular notion, but maybe an individual should have the right to take his life if he feels living it isn't possible." (CODMAN 3.1.13)

Coping with suicide is coping with death, and perhaps the time has come to change our attitudes toward both. Suicide we closet and the dying we institutionalize, perhaps to keep both from our sight. Dehumanization is the inevitable result.

Would Mr. Sullivan had leapt from the bridge if he thought he could die with some dignity at home? Would Mr. Burke have hung himself in the cellar if he and his wife had been taught to understand and accept his condition? Could we have better listened to our widows' reactions to their loss? If we accepted death, even by suicide, ourselves, we might not so desperately flee life.

"If you're reconciled with death or even if you are pretty well assured that you will have a good death, a dignified one, then every single moment of every single day is transformed because the pervasive undercurrent—the fear of death—is removed" (*Psychology Today*, August, 1970, 16).

Death with dignity even for the suicide might be our goal; concern for the living should be our continuing practice.

THE COST OF SUICIDE

THE SUICIDE OF A CONJUGANT is a life - threatening action, and it produces the most intense grief of any type of death. Some researchers call it "complicated" and others term it "acute" grief, but by any name its intensity is searing.

Seven of our twelve widows began their coping with suicide through withdrawal. Residentially, socially, and emotionally they drew back from their husbands' final plunge downward. In so doing these women behaved as perhaps most of us would have, for few among us can contemplate death and even fewer can remain close to it.

In shrinking from death these women followed no conscious design. Survival was at issue and from that level came their response. They withdrew from that for which they had cared so long—and then their husbands killed themselves. Cause and effect? Why did I? How could he?

How can I? As we observed their lives, these women had suffered much from their husbands before finally leaving them. Then they suffered additional pain.

Two of the twelve expected death but not suicide, so they too had begun to anticipate if not actually experience "the loss." Only the three remaining women, then, experienced the loss as something unexpectedly taken from them.

To the living death is loss, and our three types of widows suffered different kinds of losses. For the conjugants who were socially dying from each other's lives, the loss of one life from another (not necessarily the loss of life itself) was desired, willed through decisions that at least the widow and probably both had made. Husband and wife were in the process of being lost to each other as they separated, sought divorce, and began to build a new life totally closed off from the life as well as the death of the other.

The cost of suicide to these seven women was being joined by death from that which they were already fleeing in life. The fact that the physical death followed the social one they desired made them fear they were also responsible for the suicide, and in a way the tougher minded knew they were.

"And uh, I must admit that if we were still living together, if we were still married and living together, he probably would still be alive. Yet, for how long?" (ZACK 9.III.47)

Loss is social, the going out of one life from another; it is an experience that only sometimes includes, but must not be limited to, another's physical death. Conceived as loss, our understanding of bereavement is enhanced. No longer need we equate the moment of physical death with the beginning of bereavement, nor need we view life in its purely physiological manifestations.

The loss occasioned but not limited to death is not simply the loss of an object; a relationship, a status, and a way of being are also lost when someone goes out of our lives. The "object" or person lost also takes with him or her that part of our self that they alone maintained—our self which was a son, our self which was a mother, our self which was a spouse. The loss of object and relationship also loses us a status, a position in the social universe. No longer are we married, have children, or are known as the lost one's friend. And within whatever status is lost lies an equally lost way of being.

Bereavement then is social loss, of person, relationship, status, and way of being. The experience may be said to vary with our life's involvement with the person, relationship, status, and way of being which is lost. Therefore the cost of suicide to these twelve women varied according to their life's involvement with their husbands; that is, according to whether the conjugants were socially or physically dying, or were strangers to death. And, as we have heard, the difference was not just quantitative, but distinctly qualitative as well.

Not understanding these differences we continue to treat widows alike. "The bereaved is regarded as one for whom appropriate talk is to be restricted to 'death relevant matters'" Sudnow states (p. 137). "For what can be a long time after a death, persons tread carefully in interaction with the immediately bereaved, exhibiting caution in initiating talk about matters of general conversational value." When the death has been by suicide, even "death relevant matters" must be avoided, we think, and consequently we have nothing at all to say to the grieved widow.

"The person who commits suicide puts his psychological

skeleton in the survivors' emotional closet—he sentences the survivor to a complex of negative feeling and, most importantly, to obsessing about the reasons for the suicide death" (Shneidman, p. 22). Not wishing to hear of such "skeletons," we feel we cannot talk about the suicide, and any other conversation is inappropriate, so we leave the widow alone just when she most needs help and comfort (Gorer, p. 33). Social isolation then further endangers the survival of the grieved.

We say we don't know what to say, when what we most need to do is listen. The impact of listening is seen in our relations with the twelve widows. They had just experienced a massive shock to their entire being and we asked them to tell us about it. They did. Beginning in the first interview, their thoughts spilled forth in a monologue typically lasting several hours. They talked and talked and we listened, accepting their warm thanks for listening when they ended this initial interview.

How did you feel after we talked last time?

"Fine. It was like talking to a psychiatrist, you know; it's sort of like a mental catharsis or something." (GRENON 3.ii.45)

When Marlene Hindley and I started the initial interviews in this research we were concerned that we might have a negative impact on the widows. Several of our colleagues felt that the subject was best avoided and predicted dire consequences from our research. Even one of the widows reflected this theme fourteen months later.

"I think your study may—make it more difficult for someone to get over a death than if they weren't studied, because for a whole year they're fouled up and every

month someone comes by to talk to them about it. . . .
Time has a way—of healing things but not if you keep
bringing it up?"

What about you personally. How did you view this?

"You know, again, it really made no difference to me.
Uhhh (sigh)———it helped me THINK about certain
things. I do have a tendency if something isn't comfortable,
I don't like it or whatever, to push it out of my mind and
not think about it, and, uh, perhaps it's just forcing me to
just think about things and try to get an honest reaction to
how I felt about all these things, but I really must say I
never found any of our sessions painful or dreaded them,
or, you know, anything like that—nooo." (ZACK
14.vi.22)

Our experience as well as theirs underscored the value of
having someone to talk with.

Why did you participate in the study?

"When I first got the letter I became excited—I knew
it would be a chance to go over everything, and if I didn't
I probably wouldna thought on a lot of things so much,
and wouldna gone out so fast. Um, I was sort of happy
that someone was interested, because if I'd speak of Phil, to
my friends or something, they'd immediately shut up—
you know, they don't want to hear it, and I do need to
talk about it."

How has this affected how you feel now?

"Well, I find myself saying a lot of things that I only
thought vaguely, and through talking I get a lot of things

out that I wouldna otherwise. I think it speeded up getting over—a lot of things."

Do you think this would help most people?

"Yeah."

Do you have any suggestions of what we could do for people?

"You can't do anything for anyone unless they want it. All you can do is what you did for me—offer it." (JEF-FERSON 14.IX.8)

How do you think it would have been if you hadn't been talking to us?

"Oh, it probably would have been—that I probably would have been thinking a lot to myself and probably ended up (laughs) in the booby hatch someplace——"

How do you feel—this is the last time we'll be meeting. What do you think?

"Well——I don't know——(laughs) I don't know what to say!" (laughs)

Any thoughts about it?

"No, not really—(baby interrupts) like I said, it was a real good year, having someone to talk to——"

Do you know someone else you can talk to now?

"Well, I guess I can talk to my mother or brother."

Do you think you need someone else to talk to?

"No. No. I don't think—I don't know."

Do you feel pretty much on your feet now?

"Yep."

You've certainly been very helpful to us. We're very grateful. Do you have any suggestions for other widows like you?

"Well, I think they'd feel pretty much the same I think. They need someone to talk to——and they say time is a healer—that's true, as I say IF they have someone to talk to they get over it more." (SLOAT 15.ix.10)

We were strangers, outsiders, professionally interested in their experience and this made communication easier. Yet family and friends could also have listened and made the path to survival easier.

"What could have been different? (She repeats softly.) I think, in looking back, I think I've been very fortunate— I really do. I think I've had——several people who have been very understanding, uh, in a way it wasn't maudlin, in a way that didn't allow me to, uh, wallow in self-pity for too long. And yet they were understanding. Who were strength, but the kind of strength that not only allowed me, but slightly pushed me to gain my own strength. Uh, I think if you find, uh, even two people like that, uh, is a——I don't know, maybe other people are just as fortunate. I feel very fortunate. Uh, through all of this mess I think that, uh, I just had a couple of people around who were THAT understanding and who were that

WISE——they knew how much to shove and how much to let go, and how much to let you do on your own and yet they're there for support. Uh, so that you couldn't get ——as I said, you either could wallow in self-pity and get nowhere, and uh, nor go off the deep end too much—— THAT could have been very different. I think without that kind of thing from somewhere, uh, it might be much more difficult to get your feet back on the ground." (CODMAN 15.IX.37)

Mrs. Codman was fortunate, for most of the widows reported that their friends and relatives did not want to listen.

"Your friends don't want to hear about it. They expect you to have a strength and they don't want to—they want to be helpful, but they really don't want to see me fall apart either—you know. They're just so THRILLED that they come to your house and find that you're smiling, and that you're not crying and sobbing and having hysterics, or that you're not taking tranquilizers or pills at night, and if you're able to maintain your equilibrium and keep ——then they're happy, and they're WILLING to be supportive, you see, and all this." (GRENON 12.IX.20)

A change in our own attitudes toward death and suicide would undoubtedly provide a more supportive social fabric for the bereaved. To do this we need to recognize that everyone must be assumed to be the sole expert on his and her self. Who is to say what is best for a person except that person himself, herself? "It's not a very popular notion, but maybe an individual should have the right to take his life if he feels living isn't possible." This is not to say that we shouldn't do everything possible for all the living, even the suicidal. It is rather to accept the freedom of each, for the greater unity of all. Self - expertise assumed in all phases of the life cycle, including its willful end—that would be a worthy societal goal toward which to work. Self - expertise is the underpinning for dignity in death. Let us at least begin to work in that direction.

Programs are also possible change agents, and we explored that idea also in this research.

What would you think about the idea, which is used in a number of groups today, of bringing together people who have common kinds of experiences to talk with each other?

"Uh, uh, no. I don't think it——I mean, in my case, I don't think it would be helpful for me to meet with a, a group of people that have gone through the experience that I have. . . . I think it's unpleasant. You know."

Would it initially, do you think, at an earlier point in time might it have been?

"No. I don't think at any time." (BANKS 15.IX.2)

Let's look at some of the alternatives. . . . One would be going to psychiatrists.

"Which is too expensive—most people couldn't afford that, or wouldn't afford that——or wouldn't because they think that there's a taint of, uhh, something that— that indicates that you are a little bit mixed up in the head anyway, and, uhh—there's still, there's still a stigma connected with psychiatry." (GRENON 12.IX.37)

"I have the feeling that most psychiatrists are, uh, go along in certain fields of placings, whether it's Freudian thinking or Jung thinking. . . . Well, when my husband, for instance, when he went for medical retirement for the state, he had to go before a psychiatrist which lives down the street here, and two medical men, and, you know, this examination was to me really a farce, as far as the psychiatric examination and yet they put down, uh, anxiety reaction, you know; well I'm glad they did in a sense because then he wouldn't have gotten retirement naturally. But, uh, you know, you can pick them right out, right out of a clear blue sky. If you see six men walking down the street, you can pick out the psychiatrist almost invariably because he's the freakiest looking one you ever saw—REALLY, you know, and, uh, there was three men that walked into the office and I said to Pat 'That one is the psychiatrist,' and he said, 'How do you know?' I said, 'Wait and see.' And sure enough, you know, they always have . . ." (TIBBETTS 6.VI.27)

If you hadn't involved yourself with us, do you think you would have participated with the widow - to - widow service?

"Would I have?——I doubt it——just because I'm lazy, I think, more than anything else. Uhh, I probably would have thought, oh, heaven, it's probably too much work (laughing) you know."

If they had contacted you?

"If they had contacted me a year ago, NO, I wouldn't have." (*No?*) "No, I don't think so—not a year ago. I think GRADUALLY I would have, you know; but, uhh——" .

Yet you, you know, you picked up with me.

"Well, that was different, because I had a feeling that there was a purpose behind it, you see? But the widow -

to - widow thing, I would KNOW that this was important as far as companionship and needing other people that have similar problems and that sort of thing, but MORE of a social type of thing rather than, you know, for a REASON . . . I mean, for me (laughing) you have to have a reason (laughs)." (GRENON 12.IX.44)

If there had been such a service, would you have been likely to have gone?

"Uh - uh. I don't think so. I don't know, maybe. I don't think so. Maybe if I was depressed enough or something, I might. I don't know. I don't think so. As I said, I always had Charity to go to. A lot of people haven't got some-body. I always had my sister to go to, 'cuz she just lost her husband too. I don't know——I don't think so."

What do you think of the idea of other widows helping new widows by talking to them, telling them about their experience and so on?

"Oh, I think, like with Charity and me, she's said, 'Don't worry, it's only a phase, you're going to get over it.' I mean, anything I said she said 'I know, Sis, don't worry about that, that will go.' You know. I think that she helped me an awful lot, you know?"

What about a stranger, now if you didn't have the op-portunity of talking to your sister?

"Well, I imagine it's the same as long as somebody told you that they experienced the same thing—and it will go. I imagine that it would be the same way. I was just for-tunate that Charity, I had Charity—that's all——I think."

If someone came to you that was specifically a widow of a suicide, how would that strike you?

"If she came to the house?" (*Yes.*) "Oh yeah, yeah."

Do you think that would be helpful?

"Oh, yeah. Yeah. To talk to somebody else that had the same experience as you." (SULLIVAN 12.x.29)

I wonder if you would think about and compare these two possibilities for helping new widows: another widow helping a new widow, or someone like myself or Dr. Wallace, who have not been bereaved, but just talking and listening, and more on the basis of a formal study.

"(very softly) Well, I don't know. I'd imagine that someone that knew, that was a professional that studied it would know more about it than somebody that knows nothing about it, like another widow, she's just telling you what she feels, somebody else is going to feel different, I'd imagine somebody who studied it, he can tell you what this one feels, and what that one feels . . . and how it affects—a lot of people, than instead of affecting just one, 'cause I think that everyone is different, really, I mean, how I feel . . . the next one ain't gonna feel the way I feel, at all, I don't think. And if I go and tell you how I feel, and you ain't gettin' those feelings, it ain't gonna help you any. But if you're a professional, and you know somebody else is going through the same thing you're going through, it isn't as bad. That's what Charity used to tell me. You'll get over being mad, Sis, I used to be so mad at Joe that I couldn't think about it. You'll get over it. And you say, well, it must be true, and I think you get over it faster. Because, you know you're getting over it, you know (laughs) I don't know." (SULLIVAN 12.x.31)

Regarding any kind of community psychiatry program these widows seem to be saying that they would not ask for help—as we have seen elsewhere in their lives as well.

Was he the first professional that you kind of sought help from . . . ?

"Seek help, yes. I had talked to the home—my head nurse just prior to this but, but never to seek help—just to explain why I was acting so kooky. You know, really acting up—acting differently." (TIBBETTS 12.x.7)

Set up a program and ask them to help, tell them that they are especially needed, and the program might recruit some widows (if our twelve are representative). By their lives they prove that they will not openly seek help, so this must first be taken into account. In our research we obviously had to have their help. Their response is evident throughout this manuscript.

Other than recruitment there are a number of other issues; for example, lay versus professional help. The answer here depends mostly on available resources, in my opinion. The essential thing to keep in mind is the primary need of the widows for someone to talk to.

"There are many people who, or there are people who don't know how to listen, which is primarily what you're asking for—just someone to listen and, uh, if you're way off base, they straighten you out, you know?" (TIBBETTS 6.VI.8)

"What's the point in you and I talking if we're not going to be honest? . . . You've always made me feel VERY, VERY comfortable. I, you know, I really look forward to, to uh—to talking with you, you know. Because it was never like a doctor's appointment——I never felt that way about it. Although, you know, in a way it was, but I mean, I never felt, you know, that uh, I had to weigh my words with you or anything. Because I haven't. Never." (BANKS 14.VIII.1)

My advice to any program would be the same that I would give to any friend of a bereaved, especially one from suicide. Listen.

"You've had a lot of impact.——You really have. In the first place, I don't know if I've done you any good; I am sure you have done me good. Uh, as far as the program is concerned, I do not know how this would affect someone on a nonprofessional level. For example, if you had a group of people, talking one to one, you know, totally nonprofessional, I can't even begin to answer. I don't know how I would have related to a nonprofessional person and I do not know if I would have been so open. I think I would have kept in reserve many of the things that I feel I can say to you without even worrying about it. So that was just one aspect of the program. Uh, but because you've forced me (laughs) to take part in this, I think (laughs) I think that it was very good for me. Uh, it made me talk about things that I would not have talked about for a—for probably a longer period of time. Sometimes it dredged up what I didn't want to——I think one time I told you, 'I don't want to talk.' Uh, but it's good to get it out of your system, to the point where I can now talk about it without, you know, I'm not going to go out of here depressed, because I've discussed some of these things, but there were a few times during the winter when I did. At the same time I found I stopped talking to my sister and my attorney——I finally turned it off last summer sometime, because you can't keep it up too long, you know, 'cause it will turn them off, but having an outlet that was not just an outlet but I felt that for some reason you felt that I was contributing something to someone else. It was both an outlet and a contribution. It was EXCEEDINGLY BENEFICIAL to me." (CODMAN 15.IX.43)

Listening to someone talking. How simple! And how few do it. When engaged in, at least as we experienced it, the process had invaluable benefits. At times material was brought up that made the women uncomfortable, yet in the long run they realized the benefit.

"This, I know——but it did help me. Now, I, now maybe it was because of Mrs. Lubell [interviewer]. I don't know. But I felt like somehow or another we had something in common——I don't know why, you know if it was maybe someone else, I wouldn't have felt that way. I wouldn't have continued to come. . . . I think, uh—I think that, uh, in the beginning, well in the beginning, I mean it was torture for me to come. But as I look back now it was kind of like crying on her shoulders, a little bit. That's what it really was."

It was torture in what way? Thinking in anticipation of—?

"Oh, just to have to go through those things, you know."

Did you think about it—?

"And, and while I'd be conversing with you, I mean, something new would come into my head that I probably had never even thought about before. You know. And then, on that walk into the trolley (slight laugh) I'd think about, you know, you know, it was something that I'd think about, and maybe for a day or even two days I'd, you know, I would dwell on it. Which I didn't like but after that it was okay and then I'd look forward to coming. It was a kind of, you know, mixed, mixed feeling. I mean, it wasn't all, uh, it wasn't all pleasant——some of it was unpleasant, some of the talks that I had with Mrs. Lubell." (BANKS 15.IX.4)

Not all of the widows were equally enthusiastic about what they gained from educating us about the experience of conjugal suicide. Mrs. Zack said she thought she was doing us "a favor," and she was, but even she found it a comfortable experience. Mrs. Ago broke several appointments before saying that she didn't want to see us anymore, relented, and was ultimately grateful for the experience in our research.

In a way this research project might be considered a failure, for it influenced that which it was trying to study. If treated then solely as a program in community psychiatry, it delivered beneficial therapy to twelve volunteers at rather low cost. In addition, the project staff learned a lot; perhaps others will as well.

What does all this teach us? Once again the widows say it better than I could: "to let the people that come for you, to be with you and want you and want to be there, encourage them to be there because it saves your life, really."

SAMPLE SELECTION

Funding limitations forced us to focus solely on the deviant death of suicide, although we were also interested in exploring reactions to death by homicide and accident. The unavailability of funds further limited our inquiry to widows, although we remain eager to examine the problems facing widowers.

Taking each case as it occurred after January 1, 1970, we continued to ask widows to help us in our research until we had 16 such volunteers. The last had been widowed on September 4, 1970. Of the total number of suicides occurring during this eight month and four day period, thirty - four were eligible for participating in our study; that is, they were believed to be married and living with their spouse before the suicide, and in addition were regular residents of the Greater Boston Metropolitan Area.

Four of those eligible could not be located, even through personal field investigation beginning at the last known address. Fourteen refused to participate from the outset.

First approaching the widow no less than six weeks after the death through a letter and a written explanation of our study (which follow), the widows were asked to call us at their convenience if they wished to participate (four did so), or if they preferred, to wait for our later telephone call (which we made to the remaining twelve). In our letter and initial contact we asked only for a single interview, later evaluating each case, and assessing the quality of the relationship we thought we might have with her.

To our surprise every widow granting us a screening interview also wanted to participate in the entire year's interviews. Although we had some reservations, no one was rejected in this initial screening phase. One of the volunteers was later excluded when we learned that she had been separated from her husband for three years preceding his suicide. And although she had helped bury him, she did not know that his death has been so labeled. A second widow among the original sixteen decided she would rather not participate after concluding the third interview, and naturally we honored her request that we change our agreement with her. Two other subjects were terminated due to their rather severe psychological problems. Although we repeatedly tried to get them to seek professional help once we became aware of their difficulties, we were as unsuccessful in this as we were in continuing a research relationship with them.

Twelve of the original sixteen volunteers completed all of the year's interviews and the special tests administered at the end of it. With the widows themselves as the primary focus of attention in formal interviews conducted almost monthly, we got to know the twelve women very well indeed. Since most of the sessions were tape - recorded, transcribed, and then discussed by the staff in biweekly conferences, case comparability was maintained while each interviewer - interviewee relationship developed individually. Questions were rarely asked in a prestructured format, but rather allowed to emerge in terms of their relevance for an individual person. Interviewers were changed on two occasions through force of circumstance. And with all but two widows, the two codirectors personally conducted at least one interview with each volunteer.

LETTER TO WIDOWS

Dear ———

We are writing to you at this time to request your participation in a research project which we have just started here at the Medical School. The project calls for the interviewing of twelve bereaved persons over the period of one year in an effort to construct a project to help people when and if they want help. We feel this program could be quite worthwhile to the community which we serve. Given the opportunity to explain it more fully to you, we think you would agree.

For your information we are enclosing a description of our project. We would like to ask you to give an hour of your time. One of us would like to come to your home at your convenience to explain our research to you and to talk informally with you about your own experience.

We would like to talk with you about who and what has been helpful in assisting you in reorganizing your life, and to discuss with you the impact of bereavement on your family and friends.

We will not come to your home without your invitation. Would you, therefore, please either call us or use the enclosed self - addressed envelope to let us know whether or not we may visit you, and if so, when?

Thank you very much for your consideration.

Sincerely yours,

PROJECT STAFF:

Dr. Samuel E. Wallace

(Mrs.) Marlene Hindley

(Mrs.) Caroline Lubell

Enclosures

DESCRIPTION OF STUDY Included with Letter

A social psychological study of all types of bereavement is an essential preliminary step in order to gain understanding of the bereavement process. Such understanding is often attempted by the bereaved in an effort to come to terms with the event, but this can often be difficult. Bereaved persons are likely to repeatedly review their feelings and to distort the morning process; this can bring an added psychological burden. In the case of suicide there may also be a social stigma of the event; attitudes of suspicion could be felt from those around bereaved persons, making them feel perhaps partly responsible for the act.

The current project seeks the participation of twelve widows in a personal interview series, each interview being conducted by the Director of the study or his associates. The nature of the bereavement process and the problems associated with it will be examined. The project's goal is the construction of a community service of professional and nonprofessional help for widows, based on the data obtained from the interviews. It is hoped that this study will be of value for widows in the future in order that they may more easily adjust to the crisis.

The study should add to the understanding of suicide and of its mental health effects on the surviving family. In addition to this, the research will contribute to the development of feasible patterns of community service to prevent and remedy maladjustment and ill health among widows.

BIBLIOGRAPHY

Anderson, C. "Aspects of Pathological Grief and Mourning," *International Journal of Psychoanalysis*, Vol. 30, 1949, 48–55.

Barry, H. "A Study of Bereavements: An Approach to Problems in Mental Disease," *American Journal of Orthopsychiatry*, Vol. 9, 1939, 355.

Becker, Howard. "A Social Psychological Study of Bereavement," Master's thesis, Northwestern University, 1925–1926.

Benedict, Ruth. "Configuration of Culture in North America," *American Anthropologist*, Vol. 34, 1–27.

Bond, P. "The Psychology of Separation," *Intern*, July, 1947, 303–309.

Bowlby, J. "Separation Anxiety, *International Journal of Psychoanalysis*, Vol. 61, No. 89, 1960, 89–113.

———. "Processes of Mourning," *International Journal of Psychoanalysis*, Vol. 42, 1961, 317–340.

Brewster, H. H. "Grief: A Disrupted Human Relationship," *Human Organization*, Vol. 9, Spring, 1950, 19–22.

Brill, A. A. "Mourning, Melancholia and Compulsions," in *Freud's Contribution to Psychiatry*. New York: Norton, 1944, pp. 168–184.

Caplan, G. *Principles of Preventive Psychiatry*. New York: Basic Books, 1964.

Davis, Kingsley. "The Widow and the Social Structure: A Study in Comparative Sociology," *American Sociological Review*, Vol. 5, August, 1940, 637.

Eliot, Thomas D. "The Adjustive Behavior of Bereaved Families: A New Field for Research," *Social Forces*, Vol. 8, June, 1929, 543–549.

Freud, S. *Mourning and Melancholia*, 1917 Standard Edition, Vol. 14. London: Hogarth, 1957.

Goode, William J. *After Divorce*. Glencoe: Free Press, 1956.

Gorer, G. *Death, Grief and Mourning in Contemporary Britain*. London: Cresset Press, 1965.

Jourard, S. M. "The Invitation to Die," in *Clues to Suicide*, E. S. Shneidman and N. L. Farberow, eds. New York: McGraw-Hill, 1957, pp. 129–141.

Kennard, E. A. "Hopi Reactions to Death," *American Anthropologist*, Vol. 29, 1937, 491–494.

Krupp, George R. "The Bereavement Reaction: A Special Case of Separation Anxiety, Sociocultural Considerations," *Psychoanalytic Study of Society*, Vol. 2.

Lindemann, Erich. "Symptomatology and Management of Acute Grief," *American Journal of Psychiatry*, September, 1944, 101–141.

————. "The Dynamics of Bereavement," paper read at Annual Meeting of American Orthopsychiatric Association, New York, March 24, 1961.

Lindemann, Erich, and I. M. Greer. "A Study of Grief Emotional Responses to Suicide," *Pastoral Psychology* 4:9–13, 1953.

Marris, P. *Widows and Their Families*. London: Routledge and Kegan Paul, 1958.

Shneidman, E. S. "Fifty-eight Years," in *Clues to Suicide*, pp. 1–30.

————. Ed. *Essays in Self-Destruction*. New York: Science House, 1967.

Silving, H. "Suicide and Law," in *Clues to Suicide*, pp. 79–95.

Sudnow, D. *Passing On: The Social Organization of Dying*, Englewood, N.J.: Prentice-Hall, 1967.

ACKNOWLEDGMENTS

O~N~ BEHALF OF THE STAFF I thank, first, the women who participated in this study. Burdened though they were with grief for their husbands, they responded to others' plea for help—help in talking about a subject we all avoid, help in understanding not just "why" but also "what now." It was their wish to help us, and we all thank them for that.

Without my codirector and principal cointerviewer Marlene Hindley the project would not have been initiated, nor would it have succeeded in its data collection. Ms. Hindley was the project's only resident director for three periods, each ten to fourteen weeks long, and much of the success of the project is due to her dedicated efforts.

Research also involves the coordination of effort, and in this we were fortunate in having as project secretary the capable Carol DiNucci. Somehow she managed to maintain a thoughtful order in the files as well as within the staff. For this, and for her many other kindnesses, we all thank her.

Just prior to the first of my own travels elsewhere, Caroline Lubell joined the staff as a part-time interviewer. She worked exceedingly well with the resident staff, and I know they join me in thanking her. Sunny Karoul patiently transcribed many of the interviews; Margaret Warren contributed as a volunteer bibliophile. Cuchi and Enrique Rubiano also must be thanked for being such supportive siblings.

Phil Slater, then Chairman of the Department of Sociology, Brandeis University, contributed significantly and most generously as the project's consultant. All of us continue to learn much from him, as I did at Brandeis for many years.

My principal debt, however, is as always to my conjugant, Susan Mervin Wallace. In countless hours of discussion, sleepless nights of listening, proofreading drafts and stencils, and at least in a thousand other ways, Susan contributed.

The project was carried out at the Laboratory of Community Psychiatry of the Harvard Medical School, of which Dr. Gerald Caplan is Director. Without his foresight and leadership, and then his continuing interest and support, this project would not have been possible.

This project was supported under its original title, "Post - Ventive Study of Widows of Suicide," by the Center for Studies of Suicide Prevention, National Institute of Mental Health, Grant Number 5 - R01 - MH - 16908, January 1, 1970 to December 31, 1971.

INDEX OF PARTICIPANTS

THIS index has been charted to assist the reader. Abbreviations used are as follows: n = number; H = husband; W = wife; G.S. = grade school; H.S. = high school; B.A. = bachlor's degree; M.S. = master's degree; + = plus whatever category; N.R. = not relevant.

	Childhood, pp. 9-16					
	Birthplace	Siblings	Losses	W.	Age H.	Length
AGO Joan Bobbie	Boston	5	At age 12 father died	19	20	1
BANKS Kate George	Midwest	3	At age 4 mother died	29	30	20
BURKE Nora Don	Boston	1	None	27	31	25
CODMAN Caryl Irving	Massachusetts	1	None	37	38	3
GRENON Martha Jack	Massachusetts	0	At age 12 father divorced; at age 15 grandmother died; at age 16 father died	23	23	27
JEFFERSON Pam Phil	Massachusetts	2	At age 15 sent to reformatory for 2 years	16	20	6 months
MILLER Ann Mike	Ireland	6	None	28	36	20
MORNEAU Jeanette Jim	Canada	5	None	27	26	34
SLOAT Majorie Tom	Massachusetts	4	At age 8 sent to orphanage for 1 year	24	21	8 months
SULLIVAN Mary Doc	Boston	5	At age 6 father deserted	28	30	32
TIBBETTS Terrie Patrick	Massachusetts	12	None	44	45	4
ZACK Deborah Lester	Midwest	1	None	24	24	1

262

| Marriage, pp. 16-20 | | | | | | | | |
W. Religion H.		W. Education H.		W. Employment H.		Children	age	
C	C	H.S.	G.S.	Stenographer	Laborer	None		
C	C	H.S.	H.S.$^{+}$	Salesclerk	Electrician	2*	26	
							28	
C	C	H.S.	H.S.	At home	Manager, civil service	4	14 19 23,	27
J	J	B.A.$^{+}$	M.S.	At home	Chemist	3*	8 13 17	
P	P	H.S.	B.A.	Secretary	Executive	2	23 27	
C	P	G.S.	H.S.	At home	Post office clerk	None		
C	C	G.S.	G.S.	Nurse's aide	Painter, plasterer	5	12 13 16,	18 19
C	C	G.S.	G.S.	Factory worker	Machine erector	3	30 32 33	
C	P	H.S.	G.S.	Factory worker	Factory worker	1	4 months	
C	C	H.S.	H.S.	At home	Plumber	5	17 18 30,	31 33
C	C	H.S.$^{+}$	H.S.	Registered nurse	Chauffeur, civil service	4*	14 17 19,	23
J	P	B.A.	M.A.	Teacher	Student	None		

*Previous marriage

263

Conjugal Caring Need, pp. 20-54

	At Marriage	Later	Reason	Pattern
AGO	Present	Present	Heroin addict	Silence
BANKS	Absent	Present	Alcoholic	Silence
BURKE	Absent	Present	Arteriosclerosis and senility	Dominance
CODMAN	Present	Present	Paralyzed	Dominance
GRENON	Absent	Present	Alcoholic	Silence
JEFFERSON	Present	Present	Childhood polio; leg deformed	Silence
MILLER	Absent	Present	Work accident; alcoholic	Silence
MORNEAU	Absent	Present	Alcoholic	Silence
SLOAT	Present	Present	Epileptic	Dominance
SULLIVAN	Absent	Present	Work accident; paralytic	Dominance
TIBBETTS	Present	Present	POW; TB; alcoholic	Dominance
ZACK	Absent	Marginally	Insecurity	Dominance

Before Suicide, pp. 64-75				
Previous Attempts	W. Reaction to H.'s Attempt	Residential Separation	Length	Penultimate Communication
None	N. R.	Yes	3 months	Prison visit
None	N. R.	Yes	2 months	Gives H. half his insurance money
None	N. R.	No	N. R.	Kiss goodbye before two-hour trip
Two	Ignores and keeps secret	No	N. R.	Breakfast talk
One	Pretends never happened	Yes	2 months	At separation
One	Flees	Yes	1 day	Fleeing H.'s attack
One	No discussion	Yes	2 years	In court
One	Ignores	No	N. R.	Breakfast talk
One	Discusses	No	N. R.	Night before
None	N. R.	No	N. R.	Before going to bed
None	N. R.	No	N. R.	Breakfast
None	N. R.	Yes	6 months	H. pays money owed W.

	Face	Site	Death Method	Note	Finder
AGO	A Stranger	Prison	Hanging	No	Guard
BANKS	Social	Subway	Hit by train	Yes	Engineer
BURKE	Physical	Home	Hanging	No	Wife
CODMAN	Social	Office	Cyanide	No	Associate
GRENON	Social	H. apartment	Shooting	No	Associate
JEFFERSON	Social	Home	Hanging	Yes	Wife
MILLER	Social	H. apartment	Barbiturates	Yes	Landlord
MORNEAU	Social	Bridge	Jumping	No	Passerby
SLOAT	A stranger	Home	Drowning	No	Wife
SULLIVAN	Physical	Bridge	Jumping	No	Passerby
TIBBETTS	A stranger	Home	Barbiturates	No	Son
ZACK	Social	Building	Jumping	No	Passerby

Messenger	Viewed Body	Autopsy	Ceremonies		
			Wake, Shiva, etc.	Year's n Grave Visits	Anniversary Service
Priest	Yes	No	Yes	None	Yes
Radio	No	No	No	None	No
None	Yes	No	Yes	Weekly	Yes
Associate	No	No	Yes	None	Yes
Associate	No	No	No	None	Yes
None	Yes	No	Yes	Buried in California	No
Landlord's wife	Yes	No	Yes	One	Yes
Police; son	No	No	Yes	None	Yes
None	Yes	No	Yes	Daily, then weekly[+]	No
Police	Yes	No	Yes	One	No
Son	Yes	No	Yes	Weekly, then monthly	Yes
Cousin	Yes[*]	No	No	None	No

	After Death			
	Initial Reactions	Subsequent	Fears Insanity	Contemplation of Suicide
AGO	Disbelief	Shock, disbelief, especially in suicide; regression; digestive difficulties	No	No
BANKS	Anger	Self pity; guilt; anger at him; disbelief in suicide and death; withdrawal	Yes	No
BURKE	Shock; guilt	Goes away	No	No
CODMAN	Relief; rejection; anger	Activities	Yes	Yes
GRENON	Guilt; disbelief	Disbelief; gives care to others; psychic writing	Yes	No
JEFFERSON	Shock; horror	Vacation; disbelief	Yes	Yes
MILLER	Pity	Resumes; nothing has happened; believes suicide unintentional	No	No
MORNEAU	Mild guilt and relief	Vacation; disbelief; isolation	No	No
SLOAT	Denial	Shock; suicidal; disbelief, especially in suicide	Yes	Yes
SULLIVAN	Shock; anger	Gets mad; resents him; disbelief; privatizes search	No	No
TIBBETTS	Shock; angry denial of suicide	Depression; guilt; disbelief; especially shock in suicide	Yes	Yes
ZACK	Bitter anger; disbelief	Vacation; disbelief	No	No

Survival Tactics	Care Givers	Major Problem	Interviews	
			n	Hours
Disbelieves suicide; blocks; forms new intimate relationship	New male friend	Reminders	7	8:45
Seeks solitude; accepts self without George; sleeps	Daughter	Finances	8	15:45
Transfers	No one	Not mourning	8	11:45
Activities; this project	Sister; professionals	Rejection	9	16:50
This project; denial; struggle; eat	Friends	Anxiety	9	16:15
Fantasy analysis; acts out	No one	Fears self	9	14:45
Silence	No one	Not mourning	9	11:45
Care for others; prays for him	No one	Loneliness	7	11:15
Denial; repression; anger and transfer	Mother; brother	Raising infant son	9	12:15
Expresses anger; attempts to accept	Sister; family	Forced employment	10	11:15
Denial of suicide; seeks help	Coworkers	Accepting	12	22:00
Blocks and redirects	New male friend	Avoidance	7	8:00